Demented Memories

By

Paul Grammatico

Copyright © 2024 by Eject Press Publishing. All rights reserved.
No part of this book may be reproduced in any form or by any electronic or mechanical means, including informational storage and retrieval systems, without written permission by the author, except for the use of brief quotations in a book review. This is a book of fiction. Names, characters, places, and incidents are a product of the author's imagination. Locales and public names are sometimes used for atmospheric purposes. Any resemblance to actual people, living or dead, or to businesses, companies, events, institutions, or locales is entirely coincidental.
Keys of Demented Memories – 1st ed.

Keys of Demented Memories by Paul Grammatico
Cover by Fabled Beast Design | A. A. Medina
Edited by 360 Editing (a division of Uncomfortably Dark Horror). Editor: Candace Nola

Formatted by Fabled Beast Design | A. A. Medina

To Monji

PROLOGUE

Darkness fell about the isolated house in No Place, Louisiana, outside New Orleans, resting near the Gulf of Mexico. The two-story French Colonial sat upon a large empty plot of land with well-kept gardens that looked abandoned. The Cajun house was covered in dead silence, but this night would be alive with something deep inside the house.

An elderly woman ran down the long, darkened main hallway with several unknown figures in pursuit. She desperately hurried to the front door in panic, and the entities began to gain on her. As she went to the door, one of the shades lifted a hand with their palms outstretched, and the slightly ajar door slammed firmly shut. The woman frantically tried to open it, but as much as she pushed and pulled on the door, it refused to budge. She tried to unlock and pull it repeatedly, but her efforts were futile. Exhausted and defeated, she turned around and slumped to the floor with her back against the door; her face bloodied. As the shadows crawled upon her, she drew in her breath quickly as though in pain and lifted her hand, revealing swelling and bloating in front of her eyes.

"No… NO!" she cried.

She raised her bloated hand to her face, which was also swollen, as she contorted in panic. The shapes cast over her as she looked up, and a green substance dripped onto her as they reached their quarry. Her eyes went wide, and she unleashed a high-pitched scream of terror as their profiles enveloped her.

ONE

A WARM HAZE OF A MORNING SUMMER SUN SHONE UPON Crown Point, Louisiana, a town around twenty minutes south of New Orleans. Alexis DeLong, an average but slim woman of Creole descent who was far more wizened than her early thirties would indicate, rode in a rented silver-colored SUV. She'd made her way into town from Louis Armstrong Airport. Her grandmother's sudden death and quick funeral had hit her harder than she ever anticipated. Her mind had been riddled with guilt when she left this area to pursue her higher education at Howard University in D.C. and continued to reside in the D.M.V. area. Her gram was always there for her if she needed to talk or complain about her siblings. She was the greatest listener she'd ever had, and now she's out of her life. She always thought they would have more time for visits and catch-up sessions, but as the years peeled off the calendar, that time never came.

Alexis sighed as she turned on the long dirt road to her

house. After the funeral, she returned home in a fit of grief, hoping that it would subside with time. Unfortunately, that never happened, as she discovered she was the executor of her gram's large estate. After many conversations with her lawyer, she signed off on dividing the estate between her, her younger brother Dante, and their younger sister Kim. Her siblings told her via texts that they would meet her at the house. There was no doubt that Dante would have Jan in tow. Dante was a handful on his own, but with both of them, it could trigger an overflow of drama. All Alexis wanted to do was get this damn thing over with.

Alexis continued down the rocky, uneven dirt road where the SUV rumbled and rocked. Thank god she'd rented this car as she imagined her humble sedan's undercarriage being torn asunder through this horrid trail. The isolated house came into view with a well-kept garden on a rural dirt road with no neighbors for what seemed to be miles. The SUV pulled up to the front of the house. As it rolled to a stop, it felt like the tires were sinking into a moist patch of earth. Alexis opened the driver's side door and stepped down to the ground, a blast of humid air hitting her like an invisible slap to the face. As muggy as the humidity was in the D.C. area, it was not nearly as oppressive as Louisiana. Alexis' sweltering body and her stuck-on clothes would attest. With her hand above her eyes, Alexis turned her head slowly to the left and right, surveying the cars parked beside hers and the isolated landscape around her grandmother's domicile. *Yep, it's the same as it ever was. Not a soul within the proximity of this place.* Alexis scanned the faded façade of the French Colonial, which had been in dire need of renovation for many years. The white paint had chipped and flaked away, along with the various fissures crawling down the colonnades on the first and second floors. She breathed a long sigh, the air exiting through her teeth and lips. This place was going to be far more work than she'd imagined. She walked up to the entrance, grabbed the tarnished black brass handle of the large, heavy, pitted wooden door, and went inside, bracing herself for the neglect and grime inside if the outside indicated what would come.

§

Alexis made many trips back and forth from her large sedan, bringing in cleaning products, garbage bags, and gloves with zero help from her sibs and sis-in-law. Her dread came to light once she entered the dim, dusty house. She placed the supplies on the large, circular, solid oak kitchen table covered with dust. Alexis knew better than to ask her kin to help her, as they wouldn't lift one finger. She had to be the responsible one. She always had been. After she'd brought the last bags in, she sat on one of the creaky wooden chairs at the table and surveyed empty rooms she could barely recall from the last time she'd entered this house.

"Man, I forgot how big this house is," Alexis stated.

Dante, a man who looked far younger than his early thirties with thin features, flawless almond-brown skin, and close-cropped curly hair, popped his head around one of the doorframes of the house's main room.

"Not to mention dirty," Dante replied with a raise of his eyebrows.

Dante's sudden presence gave Alexis a start. She hated it when he did that. Dante entered the room with their sister Kim and his wife Jan. Alexis quickly recovered from the scare and slowly wiped her two fingers over the filthy table and rubbed the grit between them.

"Yeah, we should see how dirty."

Kim, the youngest in her late twenties, was slim, like her sister, with dark brown eyes, long jet-black hair, and skin the color of espresso. She looked around the house with the ever-present puzzled look on her face.

"I don't even remember this house."

"I might have been here once," Jan said. A thin, waif of a Caucasian woman in her mid-twenties, attractive but entitled, with a blonde bob and dubious demeanor, scanned her eyes about the house.

"Yeah, remember the first year we married?" Dante replied. "I brought you here."

"Oh yeah, I think I remember now. Wow! I wouldn't even know where to begin."

"Well, let's see what we've got," Alexis said, using her tone of authority.

Alexis walked to the large, steep staircase, grabbed the dark-stained railing, and went up. As her hand grabbed the railing, it felt cold and wet. It felt like the green slime toy that Dante had once placed on her when she wasn't expecting it. She couldn't stand the feel of it on her flesh. It gave her the creeps to even think about it. Only this felt like it was stored in a meat freezer. When Alexis pulled her hand off the railing, she turned the back of her hand over and looked down at it, expecting something nasty, but her palm revealed nothing. Bewildered, she continued up the stairs while the others followed her, emulating the same movements as Alexis but without the same feeling of goo upon their hands.

§

The door opened, and Alexis stepped into the room. It was a highly cluttered, dirty bedroom with dog-eared books, papers, clothes, and black mold. The others poked their heads through the door opening, catching the terrible odor of rot and decay. Each family member, squinching their face in disgust, continued surveying the massive clutter they would soon have to undertake.

"See? What did I tell you?" Dante said flatly, his face still creased in disgust.

"Yeah, it's pretty dirty and smelly," Alexis confirmed, not fazed by the rot.

"This is a bedroom, right?" Kim asked, the putrid aspects of the room assaulting her senses.

"Sure looks like it," replied Alexis with an air of uncertainty.

"If there's a bed, damned if I can find it under all this stuff," Jan said stiffly, holding her nose.

"That's one room," Alexis said with dread, knowing she would be elected to go through this putrid mess.

They left the room, and Alexis closed the door. Alexis walked the long second-floor hallway with Kim, Jan, and Dante.

§

Walking down the hall, Alexis opened another door and entered while the others followed. The next room was better, but still cluttered, minus the stench.

"Another bedroom?" Alexis said.

"I guess," Kim replied with a shrug.

"Man, she has got a lot of crap," Dante said with a groan.

"It's going to take forever to go through all of this," Jan said, whining.

"I will look around to see if there are any old boxes. See if we can't put some of these clothes in," Alexis said, scanning the bedroom for some form of container.

"You're the boss," Dante replied.

"Yeah, how come Grandma made you the executor of her estate?" Kim said with her brows furrowed.

"Because I'm the responsible one?" Alexis replied.

"Or maybe just the oldest," Dante said with a snort."Oh, now that wasn't nice," replied Kim with her hand over her mouth, stifling a giggle.

"Whatever," Alexis said with contempt. "Let's head back down to the kitchen."

Ignoring the other two rooms, they headed back down the stairs towards the kitchen. Alexis knew this was going to be about as easy as conducting oral surgery with zero anesthetic.

§

When they entered the kitchen, Alexis divided the cleaning products on the table as the others stood around. She was hoping against hope that her siblings would want to participate in cleaning this house as they all had a stake in selling the house and the surrounding property, but from their body language, her hopes dimmed.

"How long is this going to take?" said Dante.

"If we work together," Alexis replied, "We may be able to get this house in reasonable shape in a couple of weeks. Like you said, there is a lot of crap."

"Weeks?" Dante cried. "I don't want to do this for weeks.

I have other shit to do."

"So do I," Alexis stated, her voice cold. "This will have to be spread out, as I have to return to work like everyone else. I've got about a week's vacation, and I want to get the majority of this shit finished."

"This is ridiculous," Dante said as he spat out each word.

"Well, it might take a shorter time if you'd stop whining and start working."

Alexis grabbed a pair of latex gloves, walked over, and raised each hand before Dante. She pulled a glove on each hand and snapped them in his face.

"The longer you bitch about this, the longer it will take. Let's get to work."

§

Alexis became a whirlwind of cleaning as she wiped the kitchen table, returning it to its beautiful wood mahogany color encased in its original polyurethane sheen. She then placed various cleaning products in the many neglected rooms, hoping against hope that her cleaning by example would inspire her other family members to pitch in on the cleansing and purging of the neglected rooms. As she placed cleaning products in the bedroom, she looked at the ancient beds adorned with various colored bedsheets soiled with god-knows-what covering saggy, lumpy spring coil mattresses lying atop rust-corroded bedframes. Under some of these ugly beds were various storage bins of plastic or rubber coated with decades of dust and grime. *Thank god for the latex gloves,* thought Alexis. *Glad I bought a ton of them for all this nasty shit.* She pulled out the storage boxes, blew, and wiped inches of thick, gray dust from the top lid like someone rubbing a lamp in some children's fairy tale. No genie appeared, but loads of clothes from a bygone era were inside. She knew she would scour through these clothes, and maybe some would come back in style, as everything old is new again with the never-ending fashion trends. Maybe she would luck out and find something cool that would fit her perfectly.

Fat chance of that.

Alexis wondered if this would be far too much to handle and if there was any way she could order some large dumpsters for them to fill up and have some company carry them away.

Wishful thinking, thought Alexis; there isn't anything remotely close to that anywhere around here. With all of this crap in this house, Alexis debated in the back of her mind whether setting fire to this pit of disaster, then collecting and splitting the insurance money, was feasible. Provided this house was ever insured. She quickly dismissed that notion.

After she stacked the bins neatly in one of the corners of the room, she opened one of the way-too-small closets that looked to be in every room of the house. When she opened them, they were stuffed with more clothes and other ancient items placed on rotting wood and tarnished wire hangers hanging on warped wooden clothes hanging bars. She grabbed them in bunches and dropped the clothes from the closet on the deeply scratched floor.

She looked at the moldy, soiled sheets on the bed with an array of unknown bodily fluids. Her nose wrinkled in disgust for the first time since entering this house. She didn't want to find out what they were, so she quickly stripped the bedding from each bed and rolled them into a gigantic ball, hoping they could be incinerated at some point.

§

Alexis walked through the other rooms to see how everyone else was doing.

"How's it going?"

Kim looked up from putting clothes in a large garbage bag.

"Slow," Kim said with a sigh.

"Very slow," Dante stated, angrily scrubbing the blackened wall.

"How's it going with you?" Jan said, stripping the beds of their bedding.

"Not bad. I'm going downstairs to check out the only bathroom to see if it's decent, and I gotta go."

"Thanks for sharing," Dante replied. "I can't believe there's only one bathroom in this gigantic house."

"There's only one?" Kim said, her face wrinkled in protest.

"Yes, sis. Only one," Alexis replied.

"Well, that sucks."

"What's going to suck is trying to sell this house with only one bathroom," Alexis said, shaking her head as she exited the room and headed for the stairs.

"Well, hurry up in there!" Dante said with a shout. "If it's decent, I need to use it too!"

Alexis descended from the long, dark stairway to the first floor with a roll of toilet paper in tow. She continued down the narrow hallway to the heavy oak bathroom door. She opened, entered, closed the door behind her, and locked it.

Alexis set the toilet paper down on the back of the toilet

tank and looked around the bathroom. Albeit old, it had some charm to it, from the octagonal, grimy, black and white tiled floor to the chipped alabaster-colored porcelain claw-footed tub with a grubby shower curtain pulled closed around it. Alexis turned to the toilet and cringed at the appearance. The outside of the toilet was covered with black mold and old urine stains. She shook her head in disbelief.

How could my grandma let this house go like this? I remember how you could make a meal and eat off the floors of her house; they were so clean.

Knowing how old she had become, Alexis could only imagine her body breaking down and not allowing her to do the required cleaning. That, and her stubborn nature of not allowing anyone to do anything for her, was her logical conclusion for this unclean aftermath. Alexis wondered how her cleanliness would be judged when she passed on.

She lifted the toilet lid, gasped, and covered her mouth and nose with her hand due to the sight of human waste on the sides and in the bowl, which looked like it hadn't been flushed in decades. She managed to keep the food contents in her stomach, put on fresh gloves, grabbed more cleaning products, and went to work. After dumping a seemingly endless amount of bleach cleanser and what seemed to be unending scrubbing with a toilet brush, she flushed the toilet and admired her handiwork for a moment while removing her gloves. Alexis turned away from the toilet, pulled down her pants, and sat on the seat. As she released the fluids in her bladder, she admired the tiled floor design of the bathroom despite the blackened grime. Alexis thought this house was great in its day and *will be wonderful again when I finish it.*

As she finished up and reached for the toilet paper, she heard a loud sound coming from the bathtub.

DRIP.

DRIP.

DRIP.

She was doing her best to ignore the damned noise, but the more she tried to tune it out, the more the volume increased.

DRIP!

DRIP!

She huffed, wiped herself, rose from the toilet, pulled her pants up, and moved to the bathtub. Dreading that the bathtub would be a mess, she reluctantly pulled the dirty shower curtain away and looked into the claw-footed tub.

The faucet dripped into a bathtub full of brown, rusty water. Alexis screwed up her face in disgust and stared into it with a trace of curiosity that crept into her mind. She could have sworn that she saw something moving as she looked into the brackish water. She looked more intently into the rippling surface. There! A slight movement of something. Something big. She put her hands on opposite sides of the tub and moved close to it, like a child peering into a murky pond; her face and hair almost touched the water as she tried to get a better look.

No movement. She relaxed and started to pull back when she felt something cup the back of her head and plunged her face into the rusty bathtub water with a hard splash. Alexis panicked and thrashed about, unable to pull her head out of the water. She opened her eyes as the murky water filled her mouth, but then she stopped struggling and stared ahead. Her grandmother's face and the top of her naked body were there in front of Alexis. Her grandmother's eyes were wide with fear.

Their eyes met, and Alexis's muffled scream emerged as bubbles in the water. Unable to draw in another breath and unable to free herself, Alexis looked into her grandmother's eyes and watched as those eyes moved up to look at something beyond Alexis. There was intense fear etched into her grandmother's face. Her grandmother clutched her chest as her eyes begged for help. Her mouth spasmed as she tried in vain to suck in air, but bubbles escaped as it filled with water instead. Now drowning, her vision fading out, Alexis started to drift before she heard a loud knocking through the water.

"C'mon, Alex! What the hell are you doing in there?" Dante yelled.

Alexis blinked and gasped for air. She was still leaning into the tub, but there was no water. It was empty. She pulled herself away from the tub and spun around in a panic. Alone in the bathroom, Alexis gasped for air and expected her clothes to be soaked, but they were completely dry.

The hammering on the door continued. Even louder this time.

"C'mon!"

Alexis collected herself and pushed up from the edge of the clawfoot tub and onto her feet.

"Yeah. Just a minute," Alexis replied, her voice increasing in volume.

Alexis looked back and rechecked the tub. Dirty but dry. She calmed her breathing.

"I swear to God, I have no idea what you women do in the bathroom —"

She flushed the toilet, went to the bathroom sink, splashed water on her face, and washed her hands.

"What takes so damn long? You women take about ten times longer than a man. I know you have to sit on the toilet while a man can usually stand up to do his business, but Jesus Christ! It's still a mystery to me why a woman —"

The bathroom door opened, and Alexis confronted her extremely obnoxious brother.

"Dante! Really? Are you finished now?"

"Well, it's about damn time!"

"You know, you are going to hell for all that blaspheming."

"The hell I am!"

Alexis shook her head and passed Dante.

"You would think you would have looked better with all the time you spent in there," Dante said in a nasty tone.

"Shut up!" Alexis replied in anger.

§

Alexis and Jan kept sorting through some of her grandmother's things on an ancient twin bed. A large pile of garbage bags sat near the door. The pile of torn and unused clothes looked unending.

"Wow," Jan said, amazed. "I can't believe your grandmother had so much stuff. I mean, like, in every room."

"Yeah," Alexis replied. "She was a hoarder. Check this out."

Alexis held up a bunch of clothes on hangers.

"Same dresses. Every different color."

"And multiples. Wow!"

Jan, in turn, held up some clothes in packages.

"These are still in the packages."

"Those have to be recent," Alexis said.

Jan shook her head and held up the receipt. Alexis took it. She looked up from the receipt and squinted to read the faded print. Alexis continued to scan the receipt.

"You're kidding."

"Nope," Jan replied with a smirk. "Do you see it?"

"Yeah, Nineteen seventy-five. Wow, that's crazy," Alexis said, shaking her head.

"Do you think we'll finish this in a few weeks?" said Jan, hopeful.

"I don't know. If we can all work together on this, I would think so."

"God, I hope I don't get like this when I get old."

"Yeah, I was thinking the same thing. I would be embarrassed to leave my house in this condition when I leave this earth."

"I can't say I remember meeting her. What was she like? What did she do?"

"She was a lovely woman and did a lot of things. She was a bit of a Renaissance woman. Whatever she picked up, she could do well. Very gifted."

"Where's your grandfather?"

"Oh, he died a long time ago, before I was born."

"Oh."

Dante entered the room. He was holding an oversized glass canning jar that was fogged from years of grime and neglect, obscuring what was inside. A metal screw-top lid covered the entrance.

"How's it going?" asked Alexis.

"Too much work," Dante replied with a slight whine. "I've been exploring the house. Look what I found."

Dante shook the jar. It made a loud metallic sound.

"What's in the jar?" Jan said, her eyebrows raised. "Old coins?"

"I wish," Dante replied. "They're keys."

"Keys to what?" Jan said in apprehension.

"I would think to the doors of this house. Only one way to find out," Dante replied with a grin.

"So, you've done nothing," Alexis said, her voice blunt.

"I've done some, but look at the cool keys I found."

Dante shook the jar again.

"Would you please stop doing that?" said Alexis in a sharp tone. "We don't have time for this."

"C'mon," Dante said with a playful prod, "We should each pick a key and see what door it fits. It'll be fun."

"No," Alexis replied.

Dante kept shaking the jar. With each violent shake, it continued to make its metallic noise louder and louder. Alexis and Jan tried to ignore it and go back to sorting through the clothes on the bed, but the sound went from annoying to unbearable. Dante shook it repeatedly, the noise like some colicky baby demanding attention. Jan cringed in pain and put her hands over her ears. Alexis stopped working and did the same.

"Fuck. Kim!" Alexis said, her voice raised over the noise with hands still clasped over her ears.

Kim came into the room. Dante stopped, shaking the jar.

"What's up? What in the hell is that damned noise?"

"Your brother wants to explore," said Alexis with a hiss.

"I'm your brother, too," Dante replied.

"Yeah…"

"C'mon. I'm telling you," Dante said with his silky coaxing. "It'll be fun to see what keys go to what door or if any of these will work."

"Dante, please stop this," Alexis said with a sigh.

"I'll stop when you pick a key," Dante replied.

"I'm not putting my hand in that dirty jar," said Alexis.

"This comes from a woman who recently scrubbed a toilet. Come on," replied Dante, as he struggled to unscrew the lid. After many turns and teeth-gritting, the lid gave away, and the noise of unscrewing commenced.

"Dante —" Kim said in an attempt to be firm.

"And you, too," Dante replied, putting a pin in Kim's confidence balloon and extracting the lid from the jar.

"Dante! For God's sake!" Alexis said, her brows creased in annoyance. "I'm trying to get this shit done! I want this house cleaned, sold, and out of here!"

A painful pause ensued — no giving ground on this standoff.

"You finished?" Dante replied.

Alexis shook her head. Dante held out the scarred glass jar.

"Just take a break… one break," Dante pressed.

Alexis moved toward Dante and the damned jar.

"Fine."

Alexis stuck her hand into the large jar. A key appeared to lift itself to her fingers as if her flesh was magnetic. Alexis jerked her hand out of the jar as though shocked electrically by the key.

"Ow! Damn!" Alexis yelped, shaking the hurt out of the hand that held the key.

"Got static shocked, huh?" Dante replied, grinning. "Gotta pick up your feet."

Alexis looked at the floor. It was solid oak—not a shred of carpeting to be seen. A bewildered look formed on Alexis's face, but she masked it when she looked at Dante. Kim went to the jar and fished out a key. Dante moved to Jan with the jar.

"M'lady," said Dante with an edge of condescension.

"I hate when you do this, Dante. It's all about you, isn't it?" said Jan, her tone agitated.

"You know you want to. C'mon, baby. Do it for me," replied Dante in a soothing tone.

"I always do."

"You'll regret this," Jan said with a snort as she put her hand in the jar and took a key.

Alexis and Kim looked at each other in surprise. They had never seen Jan talk like that to their brother. Dante spotted his sister's exchange, his face flushed with embarrassment and anger.

"We'll talk about this later. Don't embarrass me," Dante said in a low growl.

Jan shook her head and picked up her purse from the bed. She opened it, pulled out her cell phone, and pushed a button. She stared at the screen before she smacked her cell phone hard.

"Fuck! This fucking phone won't work!"

Alexis, Kim, and Dante pulled out their phones. They tapped on their screens and stared.

"I don't have any service," Kim said plainly.

"Neither do I," Dante replied.

"Same here," Alexis said in confirmation.

Jan kept hitting and smacking her phone with her hand and against her thigh. Her face contorted into a mask of frustration and rage.

"Jan... honey. Stop," said Dante, pleading to his wife.

"Jan, none of our phones work," Alexis said, stating the obvious.

Jan continued to beat up her phone. She threw her phone down violently to the floor. The screen cracked, and the glass violently shattered outward. Jan stood over it and was about to slam her foot down on it. Kim grabbed her arm to stop the assault.

"Jan!"

Jan stopped and looked up as the others stared at her. The mask melted from her face, returning her countenance to normal as she sat on one of the beds, broke down, and cried.

"I'm sorry," Jan said, her voice breaking.

Alexis and Kim looked at each other. *What the hell just happened?* They thought in unison. Kim shook her head and left the room. Dante went to Jan. He put his arm around her and squeezed her tightly. Jan turned to Dante and hugged him back.

"It's okay, baby. It's okay," Dante said, gently patting her back with his hand.

Dante continued to rub her arm and back. Alexis watched for a moment, then stepped closer.

"Dante, can I see you for a minute?" said Alexis, struggling to keep an even tone.

Dante looked up, nodded, and turned to Jan.

"Baby… I'm going to go out into the hallway for a minute. Will you be okay?" Dante said in a whisper.

Jan nodded her head, wiping the tears from her face.

"Okay. I'll be right back." Dante said assuredly, got up, and followed Alexis to the hallway.

TWO

Dante closed the door, and Alexis turned to him. Her face was taut with anger.

"What was that all about?" Alexis hissed.

"She gets a little angry sometimes," Dante replied matter-of-factly.

"A little? You call having an all-out fit a little?"

"It wasn't that bad."

"Oh, and you're okay with that?"

"Is this a question for me or you?"

"For you."

"She is who she is. You'll have to deal with it."

"What I can't deal with is you being here."

"What are you talking about?"

"Dante, why are you here?"

"To help you out."

"No, you're not. You want to fuck around."

"Jesus —"

"You want to fuck around until you find something of value."

"That's not —"

"Something of value instead of cleaning this house."

"You're crazy."

"Am I? What did you find around this house other than the keys?"

"Nothing. Stop interrogating me."

"You've always gotten your way."

Kim approached Alexis and Dante.

"Guys."

"And you always need to be in charge," stated Dante.

"Guys…"

"I give up. You've always been a lost cause," Alexis threw up her hands as she spoke.

"Fuck you, Alex!" Dante barked.

"GUYS!" Kim exclaimed.

"What?!" Alexis and Dante yelled in unison.

"I went around and opened up one of the doors. You should come and look at this."

§

Alexis, Dante, Kim, and Jan entered the room. The large room was littered with many painted canvases and lined with large bookshelves filled with paperback and hardcover books, from classic novels to reference books. A large easel stood in the middle of the far end of the room with a canvas covered with a sheet, and a sheet over a stool with dried paint that surrounded the floor with a pallet stained with various colored oils which have now dried due to someone not putting a brush to a canvas in some time. The group explored the room in silence.

"I've never seen this room before," Kim said in a confused tone.

"I have," Alexis declared. "This is where Grandma used to paint."

"I think I remember this room," Dante said as he searched the room.

"This is what she used to do as a hobby," Alexis stated.

"Wow," Jan said in awe. "There are a lot of canvases here."

"Yeah. I used to sit in this room while Grandma painted away."

"Man... some of these paintings are pretty good," Dante said as he observed her paintings.

"She did sell some of her paintings. She had some of them shown in a local art gallery."

"Maybe we could get some of these appraised," Dante said, sensing the smell of money.

"I know an art dealer," Jan said.

"I guess we could," replied Alexis.

Kim flipped through a pile of canvases against a wall.

"I'm not sure about some of these. Have a look."

The others gathered around. Kim continued flipping through the painted canvasses as they watched. The paintings went from pastoral to more erratic and stranger with each flipping.

"What the hell?" said Dante, his face creased in bewilderment.

"Looks like she was having some issues. Did they say how she died?" asked Alexis.

"I don't know... old age? You know I don't ask about those things," said Dante.

Jan went over to the covered canvas on the easel. She lifted a corner of the sheet and peered at the canvas underneath. A bewildered look crossed her face.

"Guys... take a look at this."

Jan pulled off the sheet as they gathered around it.

"Damn..." said Kim.

"Double damn..." replied Dante.

The painting was a landscape, but a strange, dark, unknown figure resided in the background, partially obscured by paint that appeared to have been splattered on the canvas. The canvas had been damaged with holes punched and scrapes across the paintwork as if its marred features were done by a sharp object or from a large animal's claw.

"Did she do this?" said Jan.

"Must have," replied Alexis. "She lived alone."

"Lost her damn mind," Dante mumbled.

"Alzheimer's? Dementia?" Kim asked.

"Maybe, or as our brother said, simply went crazy. Can't see any other explanation."

The group cringed as they looked at it. Jan placed the sheet back over the easel.

"This room gives me the creeps," Jan said as her skin formed gooseflesh.

"Yeah, I'm outta here," Kim stated.

The group left the room and pulled the door closed behind them. It slammed hard, and one of the ancient books fell from one of the shelves and landed on the floor. The pages flipped open and stopped on a particular page, illustrating a dark figure similar to the one on the defaced painting.

THREE

Jan, Alexis, Kim, and Dante walked back along the hallway, but it seemed slightly different now, as if it bent and stretched at its own will.

"Is it me, or are there more doors than when I was in this hallway last?" Alexis asked.

Dante used his key to try all the doors in the hallway. None of them opened.

"It's you…" Dante replied.

They continued strolling down the hallway, trying door after door.

"I know I haven't told anyone about this yet, but I had a bad episode just before. I have a bad vibe about this house. I have ever since I got here," Alexis said.

"Oh no, here we go again," Kim groaned.

"Damn… not the episodes and the vibe again," Dante replied.

"Like what?" Jan asked.

"I thought I saw Grandma in the bathtub. I swear to God I did, but then she disappeared."

"Wow," Dante chagrined. "Maybe you're losing it, too."

"Excuse me, have my vibes ever been wrong?"

Kim and Dante said nothing.

"Thank you!"

Dante approached another door. He slid the key in the keyhole, and it fit perfectly. He smiled in victory. He jiggled the key but stopped as a young girl's voice came from the other side of the door, sighing.

"Dante?" the voice whispered.

"Krystal?" said Dante, a skeptical look on his face.

"Who's Krystal?" asked Jan.

"Our… sister," Kim replied, shaking in fear.

"None of you ever told me you had a sister named Krystal."

"Because she's the one we never talk about," Alexis stated in a low tone.

"Dante… why? Why did you do it?" Krystal's voice asked.

"I didn't know you would do that," Dante cried.

"Do what?" Jan asked.

§

Krystal was in her late teens, sitting on her bed and writing in her diary. Her room was bright and cheery, with everything immaculate. Her plain white walls were decorated with the latest hot male models, and a bookshelf was loaded with adolescent novels such as Judy Blume and sci-fi novels like Octavia Butler. Next to the bookshelf was a small, simple white desk with various spiral notebooks and a large ceramic mug filled with various pencils and pens. Her textbooks were stacked neatly on the wooden desk surface. She took her education seriously, and it showed throughout her room on full display.

Krystal's door opened a little, and an eyeball peered in at Krystal writing in her diary. Krystal looked up from her diary in thought. Dante, in his pre-teens, tried to open the door just a little more to get a better look at his sister on her bed with her diary. The door creaked, and he cringed.

"Who's there?" Krystal said, closing up her diary.

Dante didn't make a sound, wishing he were invisible. To come and go as he pleased and to pry into other people's things without being detected would be the ultimate dream.

"Dante? I know it's you."

"Hey," Dante replied with a sheepish grin as he fully opened the bedroom door.

"Hey. What's up?"

"Nothing."

"Don't tell me nothing. Why are you hanging around my door?"

Dante didn't reply, but Krystal saw what he was staring at—the diary in her hands.

"What? This?" Krystal said, raising her diary.

"Yeah. What are you writing about?" Dante asked.

"Nothing," Krystal replied with a tone of contempt.

"Don't tell me nothing, either. What are you writing about?"

"It's private."

"Is it about me?"

"Always about you. No, Dante, it's not about you."

"I think you're lying to me."

Dante went over to Krystal's bed.

"I want to know what you're writing about," Dante stated.

"And I said, none of your business, and you need to leave my bedroom," Krystal firmly replied.

Dante didn't move. Instead, he reached out for the diary.

"I want to see," Dante said, his tone more pressing.

Krystal kept the diary from Dante's grasp.

"No!" Krystal shouted. "Get out of here!"

Dante leaped on the bed and grabbed at the diary. Krystal, caught up in the moment of this childish play, giggled.

"Dante! Stop it!" Krystal exclaimed, giggling.

Dante grew frustrated and struck Krystal across the face with a closed fist. She fell on the bed.

"Give me the goddamn book!" Dante said with a roar.

Krystal, shocked and with a red welt forming on her cheek, grew angry as Dante climbed over her and continued to snatch at the diary. Krystal maneuvered under him, brought her foot up against his chest, and pushed out with all her strength. Dante flew through the air and slammed into the far wall, shaking everything in the room, then fell onto the floor with a thud. A female voice thundered from below — their mother.

"What's going on up there?"

Krystal looked at Dante, whose face displayed bewilderment, and was about to cry, not from injury but shock, trying to get Krystal in trouble.

"Don't you start," Krystal said softly but firmly between her teeth. "I'll tell her what you did."

Dante stopped, then glared at Krystal. Krystal turned her head in the direction of their mother's voice.

"Nothing, Mom!" Krystal shouted. "Dante tripped and fell. You know how clumsy he is!"

"Is he okay?" Mother replied.

"He's fine," Krystal said, her voice raised as she and Dante glared at each other.

"You'll pay for this," Dante said.

Dante stormed out of Krystal's room. Krystal smiled with relief before an edge of fear crossed her face as she tried to scribble in her journal.

§

Krystal's bedroom was empty as scraping noises came from the lock on the bedroom door.

CLICK!

The door opened, and Dante stood in the doorway with various tools in his hand. Young Dante entered the room and searched through Krystal's dresser. He started to throw clothing out of the dresser, and once the clothes were scattered all over the floor, Dante put his hands to search inside the drawers, which came up empty. Dante searched under her bed, but still nothing. He went to Krystal's desk. He swept her textbooks off the desk, and they landed on the carpeted floor with numerous muffled thuds and books scattered all over the tan-colored carpeting. Next was Krystal's bookshelf, and he searched through her books. He inspected each book and discarded them all over Krystal's bed. As he emptied her bookshelf, he could not find the diary. It was a futile search. Defeated and exhausted, Dante returned to Krystal's desk and plopped into her chair, frustrated. As he hunched down in defeat, he saw something under the desk. He reached under and spied a square lump hanging from the bottom of the desk. Dante went under the desk, and a distinct pulling sound comparable to the tearing of Velcro emanated. He emerged from the desk, holding Krystal's diary in his right hand. Dante saw that the diary was fastened with a lock on a leather strap. He removed his pocketknife and cut the strap, freeing the diary.

§

"Why? Why would he do that?" Jan asked in confusion.

"Because he's a busybody," Alexis stated.

"And cruel," Kim said, adding on.

"He is not. He's kind and caring," Jan said in protest.

"Maybe to you," Kim replied, stone-faced.

Dante still struggled with the key in the lock, but was unsuccessful. Krystal's voice rang out again.

"You embarrassed me, Dante. Why couldn't you have left it alone?"

"I'm sorry, sis. I'm so- so sorry."

Dante tried to force the door open using his shoulder, but his many attempts proved useless.

"Please open the door. I want to talk to you," Dante pleaded.

"No!" Krystal replied sharply.

Dante kept trying to turn the key in the lock and continued pushing against the door.

"We'll tell you how self-centered and selfish he is," Alexis said as she turned to Jan.

"And the aftermath of which he is to blame," Kim stated coldly.

§

Krystal loudly argued with her mother and father as they brandished the diary and waved it in her face. With their exchange of back and forth, with her parents scolding and Krystal pleading her case and it being dismissed at every turn, she knew this argument was fruitless, with its ending becoming a month-long grounding.

Dante's friends laughed as he held Krystal's diary, opened it, and began to read it, gesturing wildly like an actor performing an overwrought melodrama on the stage. Krystal approached them with a smile but saw that Dante had opened and was reciting from her diary as he held court with his friends. Dante and his friends turned to see her. Dante looked at Krystal with a big grin and tauntingly shook her diary. His friends snorted and giggled. Embarrassed and humiliated, Krystal ran from them, tears streaming down her cheeks. Dante and his friends continued to laugh and taunt her as she retreated to a home where she was marked as a pariah and not a daughter with nowhere to go and no place to hide.

§

A knock on Krystal's door was heard as the early morning sun of another day lit up the sheer curtains.

"Krystal? Krystal!" Dante exclaimed, knocking harder on the door.

After moments of no response, Dante managed to pick the lock on the door and pushed his way in, but stopped in his tracks. Krystal was lying in bed with some creature on top of her, who turned and glared at Dante with glowing yellow eyes. Dante closed his eyes, shook his head, and then looked back. The creature was no longer on Krystal. Dante scanned the room to see if the creature moved to a different part of the room, but there was nothing. He breathed a sigh of relief and went over to Krystal's bed.

"C'mon Krystal, it's time to get up," Dante stated.

Krystal didn't respond. Dante pushed her shoulder.

"C'mon Krystal! Stop screwing around!" Dante said angrily.

He grabbed her arm and shook it. No response or movement came from Krystal.

"Mom and Dad wanted me to wake you up. You're going to be late for school."

Dante pushed Krystal's torso harder and harder, but her body flopped around like a stuffed rag doll. Dante stopped his pushing and pulled his hand away from Krystal's body. He looked down at his hand, which was covered in blood. He looked back at Krystal's corpse, his brow furrowing in fear. Something glinted on top of the bedsheets. He picked it up and held it in the palm of his hand — a double-edged stainless steel razor blade that looked like she had absconded from her father's safety razor. Dante walked away from the bed and looked at the razor blade, dumbfounded, his terror rippling throughout his body.

"Oh, no... no. What did you do?" Dante said, mumbling in fear.

He looked back at the bed, and there it was; the creature again sat on Krystal's back and glared intensely at Dante. Dante jerked back in terror and knocked over a lamp on the nightstand. It fell and shattered loudly on the floor. Alexis, who was in her late teens, ran into the room.

"Dante, what are you doing in —"

Alexis looked at Krystal's bed. The creature still stared

at Dante. Alexis looked back at Dante. Tears welled up in her eyes. She went to Krystal's bed, and the creature suddenly vanished as soon as she approached. She gently shook Krystal.

"Krystal... Sis..."

No response came from her sister. Alexis saw the blood as it pooled in the folds of the bedsheets.

"No... no... NO!"

She sobbed and turned to Dante.

"Wha- what did you do?"

Dante opened his mouth, but nothing came out as he was frozen in terror.

"WHAT DID YOU DO?"

§

"I can't believe he would do that. I don't believe you!" Jan cried.

"Believe it or not, he did it," Alexis stated.

"You're lying!" Jan replied.

"He did. Like it or not," Kim stated.

Dante kept jostling with the key and banging on the door.

"Dante, honey, please come away from the door," Jan said, pleading.

Dante kept banging and putting his shoulder on the door as if he never heard Jan's cries.

"C'mon, sis. Please let me in. I'm so sorry."

Dante began to break down in tears. He was focusing his efforts on getting to his dead sister.

"You had no respect for me!" Krystal cried. "You violated me... And now I'm going to violate you!"

The key was sucked into the keyhole along with Dante's

fingers. Dante screamed in pain as he tried to pull his fingers from the keyhole, but he was unable to. A fast and sudden jerk pulled Dante's arm into the keyhole. Dante screamed louder as he struggled to pull out the gruesome and bloody mess that his arm had become.

"Dante!" Jan screamed.

"Help me! HELP ME!"

The girls were frozen in terror and disbelief. They tried to move towards him but could not, as if some barrier prevented them from reaching Dante as he was pulled further into the keyhole. Blood spurted everywhere. The girls recoiled away from the blood shower, but strangely, none of it landed on them. In an instant, Dante's screaming stopped, and he was gone. Blood and flesh dripped down from the keyhole that Dante was pulled through. The girls stared momentarily before realization set in, and they frantically wiped their clothes. But there was nothing on them. No blood, no gore, nothing. They looked back at the door as blood seeped out from under it and into the hallway. Alexis reached for the door and pushed it open. Krystal, who remained in her late teens, sat on her bed, wearing the clothes she wore on the day she died. The room was shrouded in darkness and decay from decades of neglect. Her back was to Alexis. Alexis ventured into the dark, dank room. As she continued toward Krystal, blood began to flow from both sides of Krystal's body and streamed down the bed and onto the floor.

"Krystal? Krys —"

Krystal flopped back on the bed. Her arms were flung over her head, and her dead eyes and open mouth came into view, much to Alexis' horror. Blood streamed profusely from deep cuts on each of Krystal's arms. Alexis, terrified, stared at the body of her sister. Krystal's features began to change into something unhuman. Horns sprouted from her head, her hair turned to vine-like growths, and her skin began to sprout moss. Fangs emerged from her open mouth, and claws formed where her hands used to be. She turned into the creature from the past. The one that Dante viewed upon his sister's death. Its eyes turned to Alexis with its tentacles that sprung from its sides, and it reached out to Alexis. Alexis jerked back to avoid its clutches and turned to Kim and Jan.

"Run!" Alexis said, yelling at the top of her lungs.

Alexis ran and pushed Kim and Jan to do the same. She turned back to see the creature following them. The girls ran toward one of the doors in the hallway.

"Try your keys!" Alexis cried.

Kim tried hers, but the key wouldn't fit in the old odd keyhole.

"Mine doesn't work!" Kim shouted.

The creature moved closer. Alexis turned to Jan.

"Jan! Try yours!"

"I'm looking!" Jan replied, her voice rising in panic.

Alexis pushed Kim and Jan towards the door, turned, and saw the beast approaching them as Kim pushed herself away from the locked entrance. As Jan continued to dig into her pockets for her key, Kim turned — her eyes met the same menace coming down the hall.

"Jan, can you speed it up, please?" Alexis said, her eyes fixed upon the danger.

"Jan, hurry the hell up!" Kim said, adding in fright.

"Found it!" Jan exclaimed.

"Try it! Try it now!" bellowed Alexis.

Jan advanced toward the door and tried her key. The key was a perfect fit, and Jan turned it to unlock the door and pushed it open. Alexis pushed them into the room and closed the door with a slam, with the creature disappearing from view, growling and prowling menacingly in the hallway.

FOUR

A LEXIS LOOKED THROUGH THE KEYHOLE TO SEE IF THE creature was still in the hallway. As hard as it was to get a good view through the keyhole, the hallway appeared empty. Despite its vacancy, fear crept through her, knowing that the creature was still present in this house.

Kim and Jan were breathing hard, with Jan sobbing uncontrollably, grieving for her dead husband. As much as the sisters wanted to grieve with her about their dead brother, they kept their emotions in check as the giant mossy nemesis in this house was their focus at the moment.

"What the hell was chasing us?" Kim asked, out of breath.

"Not sure," Alexis replied, puffing heavily, her right eye still trained through the keyhole.

Jan's sobs dissipated as she looked about the room. Her grief faded, replaced with an odd happiness in her voice, as if a spell was cast upon her.

"Oh my God!" Jan exclaimed. "It's my room!"

Alexis lifted her head from the keyhole and turned around. She looked at a room decorated with bright, colorful wallpaper of cartoon animals. A child's dresser, a large queen-sized bed, a full-length mirror, and two bookshelves filled with dolls and books. It looked like something out of one of those dreamy, unrealistic princess fairy tales.

"The room I had when I was a child!" Jan stated with a tone of pride.

Jan was mesmerized as if in some happy trance, which confused Alexis and Kim, knowing she was grieving and weeping only moments before.

"How is this room in this house?" Kim said in puzzlement.

"I don't know," Alexis replied as she shook her head.

Jan looked around the room, spinning around in a slow pirouette. She approached her toy box and opened the lid.

"My toys…"

She pulled out a jack-in-the-box and cranked the handle on its side. A pop goes the weasel tune played before a toy clown popped up from the box, and the song ended. Jan chuckled in amusement.

"Jan?" Kim said.

Jan didn't seem to hear Kim, so she went to her bed, bent over, and caressed the bed sheets gently, as if she had to make sure it was real. Jan walked over to the full-length mirror and admired herself before walking over to the small closet in the room and opening the door, which revealed a space filled with children's clothes.

"All my clothes… my dresses…"

She closed the closet door and looked around at the

bookshelves.

"My dolls! They look brand new!"

Jan moved to a bookshelf and picked up one of the dolls.

"Georgina…"

Alexis moved to the other bookshelf and took a doll as Kim wandered around the room, amazed at their surroundings. They'd never seen anything like this. Not ever.

"You named your dolls?" Alexis asked.

"Of course. Didn't you?" Jan replied.

"Maybe… I- I probably did," Alexis said, mumbling.

"I had a doll I named Jasmine," Kim stated.

Jan laid the doll on the bed like she was putting down a baby. She turned to the bookshelf and pointed at each one. Her pride swelled as if they were her offspring.

"That one's Lucy, Daphne, Mina, Clara, Dorothy…"

Jan pointed to the doll that Alexis was holding.

"Josephine or Jo…"

She reached up and picked up one of the dolls from the bookshelf. She held it lovingly.

"And, of course, Diana."

"Diana?" said Kim.

"I call her Di," Jan replied.

"Your favorite?" Alexis asked.

"Yes."

"Wow… these dolls look brand new," Kim said.

"I kept them in great shape," Jan replied, nearly boasting.

"LIAR!" said a disembodied but angry voice, spewing its venom.

Jan and Alexis looked around the room to see where the voice came from. Kim didn't react as if she was deaf to the voice. She looked at Alexis and Jan and sported a puzzled expression.

"What are you doing?" Kim asked.

"The voice," said Alexis, "Didn't you hear it?"

"No. What voice?"

The voice spoke again.

"Why don't you tell them what really happened?"

Jan stormed towards Alexis and Kim.

"Are you two fucking with me? Which one of you is doing this?" Jan said, her temper rising.

"I am!" the voice roared.

Jan looked around the room, confused. She then looked down at the doll in her hands with terror.

"That's right, Jan. It's me. Your precious Diana," the doll said.

Jan looked at the doll in disbelief. *Dolls can't do this!*

"It… it can't be," Jan stammered.

"Oh, but it is," Diana replied.

"Jan… your- your dolls can talk?" Alexis said with a tremble in her voice.

"No. They can't. They never have."

A voice from the Lucy doll emerged.

"Wish we could have when Jan was a child."

"Oh my God," Alexis said, her voice still quivering.

"What's going on? What's happening?" Kim cried. "I don't understand."

"You mean you can't hear this?" Alexis replied.

"Hear what? No! I swear!" Kim stated.

"You were such an angry little girl," Diana said.

"Shut up!" Jan replied, her voice raised in a roar.

Jan shook the doll violently.

"You shut up!" Jan yelled.

"Jan —" Alexis soothed in a failed attempt to calm Jan.

The doll that was Diana laughed at Jan's futile shaking.

"Go ahead! Shake me! Shake me all you want!" Diana said in a taunt.

"Shut up!" Jan exclaimed.

"You've done far worse!" Diana said, her voice rising.

"Worse?" Alexis asked.

The doll, Josephine, piped up.

"Oh yes. Much worse."

Alexis was shocked, stunned by the doll in her hands, speaking to her. Alexis looked at Jan.

"Jan…" Alexis said, her hands shaking, but the doll held fast in her hands.

"No… Jo. Not you, too," Jan cried.

"Why not me?" Josephine said, her voice turned hard as she spoke.

"Yes, Jan," Diana spoke in a sinister tone. "Why not her? Why not all of us?"

The dolls on the bookshelves all turned to look at Jan. Kim saw this and reacted to the dolls in shock and terror.

"Alexis?" said Kim in a whisper.

"Yeah?"

"I may not hear them, but I see them."

"Oh my God," said Alexis, seeing the movement of the dolls in unison.

"What-the-fuck?" said Kim, her voice accentuating every word.

Diana turned its head to Jan. The doll's eyes flashed at

her one-time owner.

"Tell them. Tell them what you did," Diana said firmly.

"No!" Jan cried.

"Tell them, or we will," said the doll named Lucy.

"And now I'm hearing them talk. Ho-ly shit." Kim said in shock, shaking her head in disbelief.

"Don't... please..." Jan said, tears welling up in her eyes.

"Oh, princess," Diana replied in a mocking tone.

Jan, furious, struck the doll with her fist.

"Stop it! Shut up!" said Jan, her sadness turning to anger.

"Jan!" Alexis replied loudly.

"You're a bad girl. I'm going to teach you a lesson!" Jan cried, gripping the Diana doll firmly in her hands.

"Do your worst!" Diana shouted back. "We've seen it! We've all seen it. We're going to tell this story! You're not in control; we are!"

§

Jan, around ten years old, gripped Clara in her hands, shook and hit her. She grabbed one of the doll's arms and twisted it. Jan put Daphne in her nightdress and put her on the bed. She produced a knife, lifted it above her head, and thrust it down upon the doll's head, the knife plunging through the doll's head.

§

"You've cut us with knives," Clara stated. "Steak knives. Carving knives."

"You even stole one of your father's double-edged razors to cut us up," Diana angrily added.

Something on one of the bookshelves caught Kim's attention. She moved to it and leaned in for a closer look. A double-edged razor blade lay there. Kim picked it up.

"Jesus…" Kim said, her voice coming out in a whispered tone.

"It's a lie!" Jan replied, her anxiety rising.

Alexis went over to Kim and looked at the razor blade. Her eyebrows raised in disbelief.

"I don't think it is," Alexis said.

"Oh, but there's more," Diana replied, "Far more…"

§

A knock was heard on Jan's bedroom door. When there was no response, the bedroom door opened, and her father, Geno, a tall, thin man in his late forties with hair that was far more salt than pepper, a gray-white mustache, and round, thick-rimmed glasses, entered the room. Geno looked around to see that Jan was not in her room. Geno looked at the bookshelves and saw the disfigured dolls. He shook his head and left the room before returning with a small black bag resembling a physician's medical kit. He set the bag on the floor, opened it, and removed sewing thread, needles, glue, paint, and small paintbrushes. Geno sewed the limbs together on one of the soft rag dolls. He glued components on the solid plastic and porcelain dolls. Geno picked up another doll, touched their expressions with various paint colors, then tenderly held the repaired doll and smiled. Jan looked at him through the bedroom door, which was slightly ajar—a grimace of hate formed upon her face.

Jan lay in her bed in the darkened room and listened to Geno and her mother, Miriam, a woman in her mid-thirties, thin, worn, and a bundle of nerves as her overly wrinkled face was a testament to. They argued in their bedroom, which was adjacent to Jan's.

"I'm telling you, there is something wrong with Jan," Geno said calmly.

"How can you say that about her?" Miriam cried.

"Her dolls. Have you seen her dolls?" Geno replied in anguish.

"Geno, it's a phase. She'll grow out of it," Miriam stated, knowing that Geno was right, that their daughter was troubled.

"What she does to her dolls. There's something wrong with doing that," Geno said.

"I think you're overreacting," Miriam replied.

"I think that someone should talk to her."

"You mean therapy? Our little girl?"

"I'm telling you, it's serious. She may need to go someplace for a while."

"I can't believe I'm hearing this."

The argument continued for some time in the other room. Jan got up from her bed and went to her window curtain.

§

"Your father was so loved and adored by everyone who knew him," Diana said.

"And you hated that," Clara stated.

"No, I didn't," Jan said, tears forming on her face.

"It was digitalis, wasn't it?" Lucy said.

"No! I loved my father!" Jan cried, the crocodile tears streaming down her cheeks.

"YOU KILLED HIM!" Clara roared.

Jan buried her face in her hands and sobbed in the hope that she could turn the tables from being the perpetrator to the victim.

Josephine, ignoring Jan's theatrics, spoke to Alexis.

"Go to the window and open the drapes."

Alexis, still holding Josephine, went to the window.

"No! Don't!" Jan said with a whine.

Alexis ignored Jan's pleas and opened the drapes to reveal a potted plant in the center of the window.

"Kim?"

Alexis motioned to Kim. Kim walked over and joined her, and they inspected the potted plant.

"Foxglove?"

"Yes," Kim replied, nodding in agreement.

"Jan, did you do this? Your own father?" said Alexis, amazed at this discovery.

"Oh, yes…" Josephine replied, "There's more of this story to tell…"

§

Jan saw Miriam grinding herbs with a pestle and mortar. Jan picked the leaves and flowers from the foxglove plant that she demanded her mother get at the local flower shop. She knew her mother would spoil her and provide what she wanted on demand. The snapdragon sat on her windowsill, gathering all the sun it needed to mature. Unlike her dolls, Jan took tremendous care of the plant by watering it daily. She dumped the leaves and flowers in the same mortar she stole from her mother on her nightstand and ground the plant with said pestle into a fine powder. Once the grinding was done, Jan dumped the power in her hand and closed it in a fist. She opened her dresser drawer, hid the mortar and pestle inside, and closed it with her other hand. Jan sat on her bed with her freshly damaged Josephine doll—the sound of heavy footfalls passed by her door.

"Daddy?" Jan said to the footfalls.

"Yes, honey?" Geno's voice echoed slightly in the hallway.

"Can you come here? I need some help!" Jan said, holding her damaged doll.

Her father entered her room. He held a large mug of coffee.

"What's wrong, Jan?" Geno asked.

"Can you fix Josephine? She had an accident."

Geno sat down on her bed. He put his coffee cup down on her nightstand.

"Let's have a look," Geno said, holding the arms of his glasses and pressing them up to his forehead.

Jan gave Geno the doll. Jan opened her hand over his coffee cup. Geno studied the doll while the snapdragon powder in Jan's hand fell into the large cup. Geno shook his head at the damage done to the doll. His lips pursed in pain and confusion.

"Jan, why do you do this to your dolls? Are you angry? Make me understand."

Jan became silent. Geno sighed in frustration and took a large sip of his coffee to soothe the heartache he felt for his only child. He pulled the cup away from his lips and looked quizzically at the mug, not believing its strange taste. He took another large sip, and his odd look faded as the coffee tasted as always. Geno took a moment, shrugged, and took an enormous gulp.

"Okay... let me get my bag," Geno said gently.

He rose and turned to leave, but stopped, coughed, and continued coughing. He clutched his chest and fell to the floor as his coffee cup bounced and skittered along the floor but didn't break despite the heavy force of gravity and the hard, dark-stained maple flooring with coffee going everywhere. Geno writhed in pain on the floor, clutching his right hand hard to his chest.

"Go get help," Geno said to Jan, gasping in pain.

Jan rose from the bed, stood over Geno, and looked down at him with a smile that would have made a sadist green with envy. Geno looked up at his daughter, confused and stunned by her reaction to his coronary. Geno's eyes displayed fear; his daughter had done something to him, but he couldn't comprehend it. His hand left his chest and reached out as he made one final plea to his daughter, as the light of his life dimmed.

"Please, go get your mother. Go ge —"

Geno clutched his chest again, with his knuckles turning white as he expelled his last breath. His body relaxed as he expired with his dead eyes opened. Upon Geno's death, the coffee cup and the streams of coffee on the floor vibrated. With this heavy vibration, Jan's bookcases, books, and dolls fell to the floor. Her heavy brass bed also began vibrating along the room, heavier and heavier and more robust, until two glowing yellow eyes and the creature emerged from beneath the bed. It slithered on its belly like a giant snake. Moving quickly, it climbed on top of Geno and snapped its head up to glare directly at Jan. Jan froze in terror as she had never experienced anything like the thing upon her father, not even in the traumatic books of her young childhood and would never see or read anything like it as she grew into adulthood. The bedroom door flew open, and Miriam appeared.

"I heard a noi —"

Jan turned and looked at her mother, then back at the corpse of her father. The creature was no longer there.

"Mommy! Something happened to Daddy!" said Jan to Miriam, feigning the panic in her voice.

Miriam rushed to her husband and desperately tried to shake him from his death, with each shake an exercise in futility.

"Geno? Geno, get up, get up! Oh my God, NO!"

§

Alexis and Kim remained in stunned silence at the horrific story the dolls had told them while Jan curled herself up in a tight ball, hysterically sobbing.

"They thought it was a massive heart attack," said Lucy. "They labeled it as the cause of death upon his death certificate."

"They would never have thought that such a sweet, innocent little girl like you would ever murder her own father," Diana replied with a sarcastic edge.

"Jan?" Alexis spoke with an edge of nervous energy.

"Lies! All lies! You have no proof! I would never do any of this ever!" Jan cried as the tight ball of her body unfurled, and Jan rose to her feet, her hysterics replaced by anger.

"Oh, we don't have to talk," Josephine replied calmly. "We can show what was done to us."

Josephine, still in Alexis' hands, looked up at Alexis.

"Look at me," Josephine said with a growl, "and no one else."

Black lines began to form on Josephine's face. All around her eyes and on her forehead, they were emulating deep gashes.

"No…" Alexis said in a whisper.

Josephine's hair yanked itself out violently. Alexis's face contorted with dread and terror. A scream rang out in the room. Fearing what she would witness, Alexis defied Josephine and turned her eyes to Jan in horror. Jan's countenance mimicked Josephine's as deep and bloody gashes crisscrossed her face and patches of her hair were ripped out. Alexis' mouth gaped in shock as she managed to catch a glimpse of Kim's face in the distance, which was contorted in disbelief and frozen in terror. A cracking sound came from the Josephine doll, and Alexis managed to pull herself away from the atrocities of Jan's face and looked down at it.

Josephine's limbs were pulled violently out of their sockets by some unseen force. Alexis could hear the straining and the snapping of the cords that held the doll's limbs together. Alexis looked up at Jan once again. Jan shrieked in pain as her limbs were pulled to the limit. Alexis' face squinched in disgust, along with the gritting of her teeth to the straining and snapping sounds of Jan's tendons giving way. Alexis tried to toss the doll aside, but it would not leave her hands, as if some superhuman glue held it. Cuts began to open up in the corners of Josephine's mouth and take the form of a smile that was too large and far too uneven. Not wanting to look, Alexis turned away from Jan and could only hear Jan's screams and gurgles.

"Look!" Josephine spoke in a growled and savage tone. "Look at her!"

An unknown power turned Alexis' head, and she was forced to view the gaping, hideous, and uneven smile carved upon Jan's face. Suddenly, the bedroom closet door swung open, and Jan's decayed father, Geno, walked out of the small, darkened closet, sporting the angriest look that any human being could ever attempt upon this earth. Geno held an oversized sewing needle and thick, heavy-duty thread that hung off the eye of the needle.

"Daddy! No!" Jan screamed.

Geno attacked the gashes on his daughter's face with an unnatural speed that was empty of anything mortal. Jan screamed in agony as he pushed the needle through her flesh and sewed her cuts closed. Josephine turned her head to Kim.

"This is no longer for you!"

Kim was lifted off her feet and, by some powerful force, blown backward and out of the bedroom and into the hallway. Josephine turned her head back to Alexis.

"Nor for you either!"

In the same manner as Kim, Alexis was lifted off her feet. She released Josephine, who had fallen onto the bedroom's wooden floor. Alexis was blown backward from the bedroom and into the hallway like her sister. She and Kim hit the hallway wall hard and slid onto the floor.

FIVE

Alexis and Kim scrambled off the floor and ran towards Jan's bedroom. They caught a glimpse of Geno still sewing Jan's wounds amidst shrieks of pain before the door slammed closed on them. They reached for the door handle, but the handle, along with the door, vanished and was replaced by a wall that matched the rest of the hallway. Kim pounded on the wall, but Alexis signaled for her to stop. Alexis put her ear to the wall to hear Jan's muffled screams and cries. Alexis and Kim repeatedly pounded on the wall.

"Jan?" Kim said. Her voice and hands sounded and pounded firmly upon the wall.

"Jan!" Alexis yelled, mimicking the same motions as her sister.

"Help me! Save me!" cried Jan, her pleas muffled through the wall.

Alexis and Kim continued to pound upon the barrier,

looking and feeling for a way through it. Tentacles emerged from the drywall and reached for Kim. Alexis quickly observed the sucker-lined cephalopod limbs before they reached her sister, and she moved her out of the way of their slithery reach. She held Kim close as the wall darkened like a black mold, and the creature's mossy features emerged from the wall and stared at them. Alexis and Kim turned and ran, with the creature in hot pursuit. They reached a door.

"Kim, try your key now!" Alexis shouted.

Kim fished her key out of her pocket, stuck it in the lock, and turned it. The door burst open, and the two women ran through it and slammed it behind them.

The room that surrounded them was encased in darkness. The sound of a claw brushing against a wall, digging into the ancient drywall, brought a shudder to the sisters. In the darkness, Alexis found a light switch and flipped it up. A click, and some of the dim lights blinked. A few bare bulbs in their sockets decorated the room's ceiling and shone enough light to reveal a large, dark, dank, slightly musty basement. Kim pocketed her key on the right side. There was a cellar door at the back of the room. It was a solid door with heavy, horizontal wooden slats. Holding the slats in place were black metal antique hinges with a large doorknob and a sizeable key plate with an ancient keyhole.

"This looks just like our old basement when we were kids," said Kim, still shaken about what had happened to Dante and Jan.

"But- but how did it get here?" Alexis replied in the same fashion.

Kim acted like she didn't hear Alexis and went to the

cellar door. Calming down, becoming entranced, she touched it affectionately, running her hand over the wood and metal of the door.

"The cellar door. Remember this door when we were kids?"

"Yeah. I- I remember," Alexis replied.

"I remember finding this key for this old lock around the house when we moved in," Kim said as she dug into her pockets and found the key she'd picked out of the jar. She inspected it, and within her thoughts, damned Dante with a mixture of anger and sadness. *What the hell was he thinking, dragging us into this stupid exploration? And now, I've lost him forever! We'll never get out of this place alive!*

"It looks like the key I found. Wonder if it will fit."

Kim turned the key in the lock, but it snapped in half, leaving Kim holding half of it in her hand while the end remained. Tears welled up in Kim's eyes, and overcome with grief, she fell to her knees and sobbed uncontrollably. Alexis went to Kim and held her in her arms.

"Kim? What's wrong? Why are you —?"

Alexis took Kim's hand and gently turned her hand, with Kim holding the half-broken key in her palm. The past quickly flooded back into Alexis' mind.

"Oh no... no..." Alexis said, her lips trembling. "Not again... please..."

§

A younger version of Kim and two of her young friends, Emma and Zoey, were playing in the basement. They were around ten and twelve, Kim and Zoey being slightly older. The girls sat in a circle on the gray concrete floor, with a discarded board game nearby and an old-school white MS-DOS computer on a long, wooden, rectangular table with three ladder-back chairs surrounding the CRT screen.

"Your sis is cool that she lets us play in the basement alone," said Zoey.

"Why? Don't any of your sitters let you?" questioned Kim.

"Nah. My brothers, sisters, and sitter watch over everything I do when they're around. It sucks," replied Zoey, pursing her lips with an obnoxious attitude.

"Yeah. Alexis is pretty cool," Kim stated.

"Your computer is so slow," Emma said with a sigh of frustration.

"I thought it was okay," Zoey replied.

"Nah, Emma's right. It is slow, but it's okay."

"Okay?" Emma said in a tone of protest.

"Yeah, I'm only allowed an hour of TV and computer daily, anyway."

"An hour?" Zoey said with a gasp.

"Yeah. Unless I have friends over, then it's two hours."

"Wow!" Emma said.

"But Alexis doesn't care, right?" Zoey said, raising her eyebrows for confirmation.

"No. She'll enforce it," Kim replied.

"Do Alexis and Dante get the same rule?" said Zoey.

"Are you kidding?" Kim replied with a snort. "They get to do whatever they want."

"That sucks," Emma said, her lips forming a pout.

"Yeah... I take back what I said about your sister. Not cool at all," Zoey stated.

"I know," Kim said.

"I can't wait to grow up," Zoey said in mild defiance.

They each nodded in silent concurrence without the knowledge that growing up would mean far more responsibility and that they would know this reality sooner rather than later.

"Is that why you have so many books around?" Emma asked, breaking the silence.

"Yeah, it looks like you have a ton of books — more than usual," Zoey said.

"That's partially it. But I have been interested in a certain subject," Kim replied with a tease.

"What's that?" Emma asked.

"I think I want to be an archaeologist."

"A what?" Emma replied, her brows furrowed in confusion.

"You mean you want to dig around the dirt looking for old, dead things?" said Zoey with a groan.

"Well... yeah," Kim replied.

"That sounds like fun," Emma said, disgust forming on her face.

"Loads of fun," replied Zoey, her words laced with sarcasm.

"Anyway, I think that's what I want to be," Kim stated.

"Okay... why?" Zoey asked.

"When Ms. Pritchard talked about Charles Darwin and his book On the Origin of Species —"

"Who's Charles Darwin?" said Emma.

"Life Science class," Zoey stated. "You'll have it next year. You're not missing anything."

"Yeah, so when she talked about the book, I decided to read the book and —"

"Wait... you're reading Darwin?" Zoey said.

"Yes," replied Kim.

"Charles Darwin," Zoey said again.

"Yeah."

"The old guy with the long beard that every time the teacher talks about him, makes my head hurt?"

"Yeah. I just finished reading On the Origin of Species."

"Why am I not surprised?"

"What is On the Origin of Species about?" Emma asked.

"It's about his theory of natural selection, based on his voyage to the Galapagos Islands."

"Gala- what?"

"Yeah, that's what I'm thinking," Zoey sighed.

"The Galapagos Islands. They are a bunch of islands near the equator, near Ecuador in South America," Kim stated, much like a teacher would.

"Of course, you would know that, Miss Big Brain."

"Anyway, by observing the animals on the island, he came up with his theory of natural selection."

"Natural selection? What's that?" Emma asked.

"Darwin believed that animals had to have certain characteristics to survive in their environment."

"Such as?" Zoey said.

"Well, you know how giraffes have long necks and how some birds have large beaks?"

"Yeah?" replied Emma.

"Giraffes use their long necks to get at and eat leaves on trees, while the birds use their beaks to crush seeds they feed on. They have to adapt to their place," Kim said in a lecturing tone.

"What if they don't?" Zoey asked. "Adapt to where they live?"

"Well... they die," Kim replied.

"Oh, great," Zoey sighed.

"Yeah, so I'm interested in being an archaeologist to see how some species adapted and evolved and others didn't."

"So, again, you want to go around the world and look for old bones of animals and stuff like that?" Zoey asked, not wanting to know the answer.

"Yeah, I want to do that," Kim said.

"You mean like dinosaurs?" Emma asked.

"Yeah, like dinosaurs and how, through evolution, we see the creatures we see today and how we became who we are."

"Wow. I think that's cool," Emma said in awe.

"Good for you, then," Zoey replied sarcastically.

"You're not interested in this?"

"Nah, not my thing."

An uncomfortable pause ensued between the girls. Zoey looked bored; Zoey's sarcasm had slightly hurt Kim and the lack of excitement about her vocation. Emma thought hard about what to say next.

"My daddy doesn't believe in evolution," Emma stated, breaking the pause.

"Really?" Zoey replied with intrigue.

"Yeah, he thinks that it's all made up. He believes that God made us."

"Well, evolution is just a theory. We have no clear-cut

evidence of where animals and humans came from," Kim said again in her lecture voice.

Kim and Emma look at Zoey. Zoey shrugged her shoulders in response.

"Don't look at me. I wasn't there."

"My daddy says that God created man, woman, and all the earth's creatures."

"Well, he may be right. What do you think?"

"I don't know," Emma replied. "I have dinosaur books and toys that I hide from him. He would take them away from me if he found them. I think he's right, but I love dinosaurs."

"Yeah, until they eat you," Zoey said in a low voice.

Young Kim heard this and bumped Zoey's arm with her elbow. Zoey scowled at Kim.

"So, I don't know," Emma said, ending her answer.

"It's okay. I believe in God, too, so I'm not sure either," Kim replied.

"But my daddy's never wrong. He has this beautiful Bible at home that he reads to me."

"Your dad still reads to you?" Zoey said with a frown of disapproval.

"Well, yeah," replied Emma, wondering why Zoey would disapprove of her daddy spouting verses of the holy book to her.

"Okay," Zoey replied.

"It's lovely. You should come over and see it."

"Well, maybe we will, Em," said Zoey with a slight edge of condescension.

"You know I hate that. My name is Emma, not Em." Emma replied harshly as she stood up and folded her arms.

"I know you hate that," Zoey said with a smirk.

"And I hate you when you know I hate that," replied Emma, stamping her feet in protest. "I'm leaving."

Emma turned for the basement door. Kim stopped Emma from leaving by grabbing the crook of her arm. Emma, surprised at the stopping of her exit, looked down at Kim's arm and bore her glare into Kim's eyes, her eyes shifting from surprise to anger. Kim, bringing her act of reflex into consciousness, released Emma's arm.

"Emma, please don't go," pleaded Kim. "You know Zoey didn't mean it, right, Zoey?" said Kim as she glared at Zoey.

"Yeah, yeah, I didn't mean it. I'm sorry. God, chill out," replied Zoey.

Emma, satisfied with the apology, returned to her place in the circle. Her anger faded into happiness as if the angry exchange never took place.

"Wow, I felt like you were simultaneously channeling parts of my brother," Kim said, draining the remaining tension from the group.

"Eww!" Emma said, her face creased in a grimace.

"I think your brother's handsome," said Zoey.

"Eww!" Kim and Emma shouted in unison.

"Not me. He wears too much perfume," Emma said.

"It's not perfume," Kim replied. "It's cologne. That's what men wear."

"Whatever it is, it stinks," Emma said in disgust.

"I think he smells great."

"Ewww!" Kim replied with the same crease of revulsion.

"What? Why can't you find your brother attractive?" Zoey replied in defense of her feelings for Dante.

"You're kidding me!" said Kim.

"One day, he will fall in love with me," replied Zoey dreamily.

"You are dreaming," Kim said.

"You'll see."

"Ewww!" Emma replied in distaste.

"We're going to get married someday."

"EWWW!" Emma and Kim said in unison.

Kim pushed Zoey towards the cellar door. She nodded to Emma to open the door.

"I'm telling you, you'll see," Zoey stated in a futile attempt to convince her friends of this reality.

"Ewww! So gross!" Kim replied.

Emma opened the cellar door. Kim pushed Zoey into the dimly lit cellar, and they shut the door on Zoey. Kim produced a key from her pocket and locked the door. The two girls laughed as Zoey pushed against the door, but it didn't budge. She tried the doorknob. It turned, but the door refused to open.

"Hilarious, you guys!" Zoey yelled behind the door as she banged on it, "I'm sorry you two can't handle the truth."

Zoey heard laughing behind the door. Zoey banged on the door, emanating a thud of wood and metallic clanging from the wooden slats and metal hardware. She rattled the doorknob, but her exit was refused.

"Okay, you two," said Zoey as if she was the adult in the room.

Zoey searched for a wall or pull switch in the cellar. A tiny light stream came from a high vent in one corner where the ceiling and the floor intersected. She spied large wooden shelves filled with the shadows of large mason jars holding god-knows-what inside them. The liquid that co-habited the numerous objects within the mason jars glowed from the dim vent light, creating a ghostly and unsettling atmosphere for Zoey.

"This isn't funny anymore!" Zoey called out.

She rattled the doorknob again and pushed against the door, but the door refused to budge.

"You need to let me out," Zoey said, her anxiety starting to rise.

In the far corner of the cellar, something dark and slightly human-looking was curled up in the blackness. In the dim light, the thing was covered in green fur that Zoey had seen on trees and rocks during the summer. The creature began scratching upon the cinderblock walls, which brought rapid breathing from Zoey. She wasn't sure if she saw this creature for real or some figment of her imagination coupled with the dark.

"It's dark and creepy in here," Zoey said, her anxiety mixing with fear.

Zoey coughed and wheezed. She patted her empty pockets and then looked around in the dim light, panicking. She dropped to her knees and swept her hands across the cold stone floor. Zoey's coughs and wheezes grew louder. She desperately pounded on the door. Her need to escape from her prison grew more and more desperate.

Kim and Emma were still giggling on the other side of the cellar door. They heard Zoey's pounding, and both placed their ears on the door. They heard Zoey's coughing and wheezing getting louder and more often. They looked at each other and rolled their eyes. They knew that Zoey had an affinity for exaggeration and a flair for the dramatic. She also had asthma, but Kim felt that she would overplay her illness to the point of an extreme hypochondriac. As Kim and Emma stepped away from the door, Kim kicked something with the back of her heel, making a plastic and aluminum clink on the stone floor. She looked back to view an asthma inhaler on the floor — Zoey's asthma inhaler. Kim's eyes went wide with shock and surprise. She snatched the inhaler with one hand, dug the key out of her pocket, and raced to the cellar door.

"What's wrong?" Emma asked, "Why are you —"

Emma saw the inhaler in Kim's hand. She went to the door. Kim put the key into the lock and twisted it hard. The key snapped off in the lock, leaving her with the broken end in her hand. Emma turned the doorknob, but it refused to open. Kim and Emma started banging on the door frantically.

"Zoey!" Kim yelled. "Talk to me."

But Zoey could only cough and wheeze, muffling her speech and the ability to form words for help.

"Zoey, Zoey!" Kim said, her voice rising in fear.

Hurried footsteps of quick, soft thuds came down the basement steps. The seventeen-year-old Alexis rushed to Emma and Kim as they banged, screamed, and pulled at the door.

"What's going on?" shouted Alexis in a panicked tone.

"Zoey is having an asthma attack!" said Kim at the top of her lungs.

Kim showed Alexis the inhaler in her hand. Alexis took the inhaler from Kim and looked at the label, revealing it was Zoey's.

"She's in the cellar!" Kim cried, tears forming in her eyes. "I locked her in!"

Alexis rattled the doorknob and pounded on the door.

"Zoey? Zoey!" Alexis shouted at the door as she rattled the doorknob and pounded. "Kim, where's the key to the door?

Kim showed her the half-broken key in her hand. Alexis grabbed the key to get a better look. Panic and fear gripped Alexis. Their mother always told them that it was only fun until someone lost an eye, but, in this case, this is far more than an eye.

"Oh no... no, no, no! Shit!"

Alexis ran off. Emma and Kim banged on the door. They screamed and cried, trying in vain to open the door. Alexis returned, holding a fire axe, determined to get to Zoey by any means necessary and that she was alive on the other side.

"Kim! Emma! Get away from the door!" Alexis bellowed.

Emma and Kim moved quickly away from the door. Due to the axe's size and weight, Alexis side-swung the axe into the door.

THUNK!

As Alexis swung repeatedly, the blade of the sharp axe chewed into the wood bit by bit until wooden slats splintered and finally broke apart, creating a hole big enough for Alexis and the two girls to fit through. Alexis rushed to Zoey, who was unconscious and lying on the floor on her side. Alexis managed to reach Zoey and began to shake her, but her shakes proved fruitless as Zoey lay unresponsive. Alexis flipped Zoey onto her back, grabbed her inhaler from her pocket, and put it into Zoey's mouth. Alexis pushed down on the inhaler, and the mist attempted to enter Zoey's lungs.

"C'mon, Zoey! C'mon! Breathe! Breathe it in!" Alexis said urgently, still trying to shake Zoey awake.

Alexis kept pushing the inhaler down again and again with the mist entering Zoey's mouth, but the massive effort proved futile as Zoey's lips and face were drained of color. Alexis attempted mouth-to-mouth resuscitation. After many breaths of life from Alexis, she put her ear to Zoey's chest. Alexis stopped her CPR and looked at Emma and Kim in defeat–their friend was dead. Tears welled up in Alexis's eyes, and she wept gently. Kim and Emma stared in disbelief. They shook their heads and they both burst into uncontrollable tears. Kim looked up from the dead Zoey and saw two glowing, strange, and terrifying yellow eyes in the darkness through her blurry vision because of the watery discharge of her guilt.

§

BANG!

The noise that emerged from the door shook Kim from the horrific daydream of her past. She felt her face, and the same liquid discharge emerged. She wiped her eyes and looked at the cellar door as it vibrated with the repeated banging.

BANG! BANG!

"Kim…" Alexis said.

Kim turned and saw Alexis holding the same large axe she'd used all those years ago.

"How did you find —"

"In the same place, it's always been."

Alexis motioned with her hand, and Kim got to her feet and moved away from the same cellar door at their childhood home with its wooden slats and metal accoutrements. Alexis went to the door and swung the axe. It crashed into the door, the wood slats splintering as the sharp blade of the heavy axe went into it more deeply than before, with the metal vibrating with each blow. Alexis used her more muscular strength now that she was an older woman. She continued swinging into the door until pieces fell to the floor, the hinges gave way, and the remains slammed onto the cold stone floor. Kim and Alexis looked into the dark cellar. A small shape stood up in the back of the cellar and emerged from the dark – Zoey just as she was when she was twelve years old, wearing the same clothes on the day of her death.

"Oh my God... Zoey..." Kim said, barely able to get the words out.

Zoey stood in the doorway. Behind her were two glowing yellow eyes glaring at Alexis and Kim in the far back of the cellar.

"So... you've come back. Why?" Zoey said in a demanding tone.

"I don't know..." Kim replied. "We came into this room because some strange creature was chasing us. This room is in my grandmother's house."

"I see you're all grown up. Wish I had that chance," Zoey replied as she looked Kim up and down.

"Zoey," Kim whimpered, "I'm so sorry. I didn't mean —"

"But growing up never happened for me, did it?"

"Zoey —"

"Because you killed me!"

"She didn't kill you," Alexis said. "It was an accident!"

Alexis' eyes narrowed as she looked at the large glowing yellow eyes behind Zoey. She surmised that the creature standing behind her was at least seven-foot tall with the same attributes as the beast that terrorized them throughout the house.

"Who's your friend?" Alexis asked.

"You wouldn't know about him. But you should," Zoey replied with a growl, then turned her attention to Kim. "You should pay for what you did to me."

"You girls were playing, and the key broke off in the lock," Alexis stated. "It happens."

"It didn't have to if Kim didn't lock me in with an old key. Stay out of it," Zoey replied with a roar. "This is not your fight!"

"Not my fight?" Alexis said, her anger rising. "I was the one who broke the door down and tried to save you!"

"Yeah, you tried to save me but didn't, so stay out!" Zoey replied as she turned her head back to Kim, her eyes blazing with anger.

"So, you're sorry? Tell me another lie, you murdering whore!"

"Don't say that to her!" Alexis said.

"No, she's right," Kim stated in a low tone that was nearly inaudible.

"What?" Alexis replied, shocked at her sister's compliance.

"She's right. I am a murderer," Kim said.

"You're not," Alexis replied in objection.

"I am."

Kim turned towards Zoey.

"You have every right to call me whatever you want. The day you died was the day I no longer wanted to live," Kim said, as if she was in a confessional. She took Alexis' hand and placed it in hers. "Remember?"

§

Kim stood before the replaced cellar door, its features mimicking the destroyed one. Kim, staring at the door like some religious shrine, fell to her knees and sobbed violently. Kim held a glass of water in one hand and a handful of multi-colored pills of all shapes and sizes in the other. She dumped all the pills into her mouth. With her mouth full, Kim attempted to take gulps of water to swallow down the mountain of pills, but the amount was far too large. Water and pills spewed out of Kim's mouth, and she coughed violently in her suicide attempt. The glass of water in her hand slipped from her grip and smashed to pieces on the gray stone floor.

"Kim?" Alexis said in a raised tone from the floor above.

Alexis quickly descended the stairs, turned, and saw Kim prostrate. Alexis craned her head to see the pool of water and pills. Alexis approached and knelt beside Kim to better look at the water, pills, and shards of glass from Kim's failed attempt. Alexis' mouth gaped open in surprise. She reached out and tenderly touched her sister.

"What's going on down there?" their mother shouted at them from the upper floor.

"It's me, Mom. I dropped an old mason jar in the cellar," Alexis shouted up at her as she jumped in surprise at her voice. "I'm sorry. I'll clean it up."

An angry but inaudible rant from their mother was heard upstairs. Alexis curiously looked at the mess on the floor and her sister. She stared into her troubled eyes.

"Don't... please don't," Kim begged.

"I won't... I love you," Alexis said in a soft tone.

They both broke down in tears. Alexis held Kim in her arms in a firm but loving embrace, their despair flowing between them. Kim broke their hug, lowering and shaking her head from the love she didn't deserve.

"I- I can't," Kim spoke through her tears.

"You can," Alexis replied in a soothing voice.

"I don't want to be here," Kim said.

"I know... but I don't want you to go."

"It's my fault... all my fault."

"Kim..."

"I should be —"

"Shhh. You shouldn't punish yourself like this."

"You're wrong. I should. I can't sleep, I can't eat," Kim sobbed.

"You've been eating when we're at dinner," Alexis stated.

"I've forced myself. I don't want Mom and Dad to know."

A long, grieving pause ensued between the two sisters until Alexis looked at the pills on the floor.

"The pills?" asked Alexis.

"Vicodin and Nembutal. From Dad's surgery and Mom's insomnia. They left them in the medicine cabinet."

"How did you get —"

"I took a couple at a time every day and stored them. Mom doesn't keep track, and Dad doesn't take his."

"But with what happened to Krystal and her—"

"I know. When she did that, I told myself I would never

do what she did. That whatever happens to me, I will be able to overcome it. Yet here I am."

"But Dante drove her to it," Alexis said with insistence. "He has to live with that. What you did wasn't even close."

"But it's the same result, isn't it?" Kim replied.

"Kim, you can't keep blaming yourself for this," Alexis said.

"But I do, every day. It haunts me all the time."

"Kim —"

"Why shouldn't it?"

Alexis opened her mouth to speak, to persuade and soothe Kim's pain of guilt, but she was speechless, unable to say anything of substance.

"All the time…" Kim said with a sigh.

"What can I do to help?" said Alexis, still trying to think of something… anything.

"You can't," Kim replied.

"I can. I want to," Alexis softly spoke.

"Why?"

"I wasn't there for Krystal. I failed her. I don't want to fail you."

"You want… redemption?"

"I guess you could say that. I didn't help Krystal like I felt I should have. I want to help you. To be there for you."

Alexis reached out and gave Kim another embrace but more lifeless, with her sister's body becoming limp in her arms.

"You're my baby sister. I love you," Alexis said.

"I'm not a baby anymore."

"I know."

"I- I don't know if it's possible to save me," Kim said, her lips trembling as she spoke.

"I know one thing we can do for now."

Alexis got up, walked off, and returned with a whisk, broom, and a dustpan. She knelt beside Kim to sweep the pills, water, and glass shards.

"No one ever needs to know about this," Alexis said in assurance.

With her eyes pooled with tears, Kim turned to Alexis and pulled her sister into a hug filled with vitality and love, which was returned with the same spirit.

§

"I didn't try to end my life again," Kim stated to Zoey and the yellow-eyed creature behind her. "I thought about it all the time but never went through with it. I guess I didn't have the nerve."

"You were weak," Zoey replied with a snort.

"You were my best friend," Kim said. "We told each other everything."

"I even told you about my asthma," Zoey replied, her voice sharpening each word.

Alexis looked at Kim in surprise. Kim silently bowed in ignorance and shame, knowing Zoey was right.

"Why would you lock me in the cellar like that, knowing I had asthma?" Zoey said.

"Because I wanted to treat you like everyone else," Kim replied. "People treated me differently because of who I was and my interests, and I didn't want to do that to you because you had some condition."

"You never knew my condition could be fatal, did you?"

said Zoey in a savage tone.

"I didn't. I didn't think it was that serious an illness. I'm sorry," replied Kim.

"All those books you read and not one about your best friend's illness. Your ignorance didn't save you then, and it won't save you now."

"I know."

Zoey walked back into the cellar and the darkness, never to return. The two glowing yellow eyes glared at Kim from the dark. Kim lowered her head and waited for the punishment of her death, but nothing happened.

"Nothing..." Alexis said in a soothing voice. "They can't touch you because you admitted your guilt and are truly sorry. You're free."

Alexis walked towards the darkness and confronted the glowing yellow eyes.

"You lost!" Alexis said, crowing in victory. "You would never do anything to my sister! I was never going to let you! You hear me, you stupid asshole? You're not going to do a goddamn thing!"

The yellow eyes moved closer and closer to the cellar door. The shaggy shape came into view from the shadows and ran straight toward Alexis and Kim. Alexis turned and ran towards the basement room exit. She turned to look for Kim, but Kim knelt in front of the cellar door, now sealed up as if it was resurrected from Alexis' destruction. The creature ignored Kim and was hot on Alexis' heels. Alexis opened the door and made her escape into the hallway with the creature behind her.

Alexis ran down the hallway and reached the door

where her grandmother's paintings resided. She tried the door, but this time, it refused to open. She removed her key from her pocket and quickly shoved it into the keyhole. It fit. Alexis turned the key and opened the door. As the creature advanced towards the room's entrance, Alexis entered quickly and slammed the door behind her.

SIX

ALEXIS PROPPED HERSELF AGAINST THE DOOR AND PANTED heavily with panic and confusion about what had happened in the room with Kim and how the cellar door had been restored. She debated whether to stay in this room to protect herself, venture out into the hallway, battle the creature, and return to save her sister.

"Come here, child," an elderly female voice drifted through the air like a gentle breeze.

Stunned and terrified by the sweet and familiar voice, Alexis stiffened but desperately held her position, not turning around to view what was creating the voice she knew came from the deceased.

"Alexis Ann!" the voice cried. "I know you can hear me. Turn around and face me. I want to talk to you."

Alexis hugged the door, shuddered, and, as she turned to see what made the voice with her own eyes, she shook her head incredulously. There she was, her grandmother Shirley

Chapman, a thin slip of a woman whose tight, cocoa-brown skin dotted with several small age spots which enhanced her beauty and made her look decades younger than she was, although she would never let anyone on about her actual age. Her straight, gray hair was tied neatly in a tight bun with a ribbon of azure encircling its perfect shape. Dressed in a simple housedress of beige and red, she hummed a few bars of a gentle tune that eased Alexis' anxiety and placed her in a gentle trance. Shirley quietly stopped her honeyed voice and looked upon the grown Alexis.

"You always liked that tune as a child. It always soothed you," Shirley said, her voice light as a feather falling to the floor.

Shirley resumed humming that beautiful, soothing tune in her sweet voice. Alexis slowly turned to Shirley, who sat on her stool in front of a canvas on an easel and added to the painting with a brush and palette. Alexis watched her momentarily before she turned and put her right eye into the keyhole, which revealed nothing. Alexis put her ear to the door and listened. Again, nothing.

"It's okay, child. No harm will come to you," Shirley said.

Alexis turned back to face her grandmother. Strangely, she wasn't afraid, but the disbelief at seeing her at her easel like she did as a child remained.

"Gram, what are you doing here?"

"Well… this is my house, dear. You know that."

"I know, but you're —"

"I know, baby, but this is my home, and I'm here. I'll always be here."

Shirley goes back to fixing a damaged painting.

"What are you doing?"

"The Mal un Marais. They don't want to be included in my paintings."

Alexis walked toward her grandmother while dodging some of the various paint splatters that had accumulated on the floor.

"The Mal un Mar —"

In her attempt at navigating the obstacle course of colors, Alexis accidentally kicked the book onto the floor. The same one that fell when she, her siblings, and her sis-in-law exited this room for the first time. Alexis looked down at it. The illustration of the creature that had tormented them throughout this adventure was displayed in a crude sketch on the open page. The picture's most prominent feature depicting the creature, amongst its tall, heavy frame, mossy growth upon its exterior, and flowing tentacles out of its sides, was the glowing yellow eyes. Alexis looked at her grandmother, who pointed at the book on the dusty floor. Alexis picked up the book, placed both hands on the cover, and carefully brought the book closer to her to make the print and graphics decipherable to her sight. Shifting her right hand from the cover to the book's spine to ensure better balance, Alexis stared intently into the book, her eyes fixated on the illustration of a creature whose name was unknown, but its presence was a constant terror she could attest to within the house.

"Read to me, child," Shirley said with pleasure in her voice.

Alexis shifted her focus from the illustration to the yellowed pages of the ancient book and read the block black text aloud.

"The Mal un Marais are shape-shifting demons that reside in bog or marshland areas. They allegedly have been seen in parts of coastal Louisiana around the Gulf of Mexico and parts of the Everglades regions of southern Florida, where the locals call it the Malvados Pantanos. They are considered trickster demons who can change their bodies at will. Their origins are believed to be from one of the many levels of Hell, but that has yet to be confirmed. Their role within Hell is said to be that of punishers who torment and torture the souls that have been damned in the spiritual world for their crimes in the material world, but none of this has been determined. Their vulnerabilities and weaknesses are not known at this time."

"There's more. Come and sit with me."

Alexis read while moving towards the easel. Her grandmother listened while fixing the damage and painting a pastoral scene with her various colored oils.

"The Mal un Marais can take the shape or enter the body of humans. Certain people can summon these creatures needing their services by simply praying. These demons can only be viewed and utilized by humans with a clairvoyant trait or what is known as 'sight.' Other people who do not possess this trait but are in the presence of a 'sighted' person can also view these creatures."

Alexis looked up from the book and finally realized for the first time what these inhuman creatures were and how they could change into something human from unholy.

"Gram, do I —"

"You see them, don't you?" asked Shirley.

"Yes," Alexis replied.

"And others can see them in your presence?"

"Yes."

"Then you do. I can see them too. Come sit with me."

Alexis put the book down, went to her grandmother, sat on the floor, and crossed her legs. Her grandmother looked down from her chair and smiled at her.

"You sit the same as you did as a child. So efficient and proper," Shirley stated proudly as she turned and continued to fix her painting.

"Why did they not want to be in the paintings? Are they afraid of people finding out about them?" Alexis asked, pointing at the damage.

"No, not really. They like to cause trouble and display their petty torments to annoy me. They've done this to a number of my canvases. Some I've been able to fix. The others, well…"

"Have they always been here?" asked Alexis, digging into her mind to recall if she ever remembered these creatures from her past visits.

"Not always. You don't remember them, do you?"

§

Shirley knelt in her garden with her hands clasped together in prayer. She looked up at the sky. Her hands were still clasped in prayer. Noises were heard from the ground, but Shirley remained focused on the heavens above. She closed her eyes tightly and prayed harder. The sound of her sod being ripped apart in front of her broke her concentration, and she looked down at the ground. Shirley saw numerous creatures emerge from the lawn near her knees, opening a large patch of grass and pushing it to the side like a manhole cover. More and more of these unknown entities pulled themselves out of the dirt. A mixture of shock and pleasant surprise crossed Shirley's face, but when she realized that these beings were her manna from 'heaven,' her surprised face melted into a smiling one.

§

"I prayed for someone to help me," Shirley said flatly, applying her brush to the marred canvas. "Sometimes, you don't get exactly what you pray for. But you take what you can get."

"Why were you praying for help?" Alexis asked, confusion crossing her face.

"I was afraid I would be taken out of my home," Shirley stated.

"Why?"

"It was just a feeling I had."

§

Shirley walked through the house and flipped through the mail she'd retrieved from the outside mailbox. When Shirley reached the circular wood mahogany table, worry and frustration crossing her face, she went to the kitchen table. She dropped each envelope upon a pile of envelopes marked with red 'Second Notice' stamps, replacing them with red ' Final Notice' stamped envelopes. The last envelope came from the City Tax Board, joined by the other with a red stamp, 'Final Notice.' She sat, placed her head in her hands, and was on the verge of weeping as she was helpless to come up with the funds to deal with her predicament. Shirley suddenly straightened herself out and looked at the pile of overdue property tax letters and other overdue bills. She picked up each pile and began tearing each letter up individually. When she finally completed the destruction of her bills, she gathered the scraps of paper and dumped them in the trash.

§

"Really?" asked Alexis, wondering how her grandmother got into such arrears and why she never asked for help.

"Yes," Shirley replied. "I was getting older and alone. People always think that old people need help, and often we don't, but sometimes we do."

"Why didn't you ask me? I would have helped you, or we could have worked something out."

"I didn't want to be a bother to you. Besides, I had no idea how I would reach you. It's been a long time. Too long."

Alexis bowed her head, embarrassed at the neglect of her grandmother. She cursed herself for not visiting her more often. She loved and adored her grandmother and, being the oldest granddaughter, felt that she had a responsibility to help her out. Life be damned!

"And that's why you prayed?" Alexis said in an attempt to shake off her guilt.

"Yes, and it was answered," Shirley replied as she tapped on the book that was now crooked under Alexis' arm. "They came."

"Why haven't I seen them before?" said Alexis, racking her brain to remember these creatures.

"You saw them as a child. I'm surprised you don't remember," replied Shirley, recalling when she and Alexis, then a tiny child, discussed the Mal un Marais. Shirley wished she'd been more forthcoming when these creatures roamed this estate.

§

Shirley was wearing garden gloves and kneeled to fix the divots on her front lawn courtesy of the Mal un Marais group. A shovel and a bag of grass seed were nearby. She patted down several large grass patches into their original positions. Alexis exited Shirley's house at about eight years old and knelt with Shirley in the grass.

"Whatcha doin', Gram?" Alexis asked, sing-song.

"I'm just gardening, dear," Shirley replied in a gentle voice.

"That's not gardening," Alexis stated.

"It's not?" said Shirley.

"That's grass, not plants."

"Grass is a plant, too, child. It's just different," Shirley said, chuckling at Alexis.

"Why are you gardening the grass?"

"Something damaged the grass, and I'm trying to return it to how it was."

"Is it gophers?" Alexis asked.

"Gophers?"

"Yeah, we have gophers in our backyard, which damages our grass," Alexis stated.

"Oh... really?"

"Daddy said some bad words when he saw the gophers. He said I couldn't repeat them."

"No, it's not gophers, honey."

"Is it moles?" Alexis said, looking intently at the holes.

"Well, no... not quite," Shirley replied.

§

"I should have been clearer when you were younger, but I feared you wouldn't understand. I didn't want to frighten you."

"They were around when I was a child? And I saw them?"

"Yes. The creature under your bed, the monsters you claimed you saw in the walls and ceilings, your imaginary friend you would talk to when you spent time here as a child. That was them."

"Why don't I remember this?"

"No doubt because it's been long since you were here. You're a grown, mature woman now. I can't believe how long it's been. How I've missed you."

As her grandmother's words moved her, tears welled up in Alexis's eyes.

"Gram... I- I'm sorry. I should have seen you."

"I know, child, but the Mal un Marais have kept me company for all these years. They've been a great help for many years. I vividly recall one of those times."

§

Shirley tended to her various plants out in front of the house. She wore an apron and gardening gloves. A costly luxury car pulled up in front of the house, and a well-dressed, middle-aged Caucasian man of fifty climbed out of his vehicle. His squatty frame made him look far shorter than he was. He was sharply dressed, clad in a far too-expensive suit and designer footwear. This man did not simply stand out like the typical sore thumb, but more of a puffy, blister-scabbed one. Shirley glanced over at the man but then resumed tending to her plants as the man approached her.

"Shirley? Shirley Chapman?" the man asked.

"Yes?" said Shirley, not looking up.

"My name's Jack, Jack LaForge."

He offered his hand. Shirley looked at it, then clasped it with her dirty glove and shook LaForge's hand. LaForge looked at his dirty hand when she finally released it. He smiled and chuckled in an awkward defensive posture as he clapped his hands together and dusted them off as best he could, and Shirley returned to tending to her plants.

"Yes, well, I'm the treasurer and tax assessor for the town. May I speak to you for a minute?" he asked, his voice stiff as an over-starched shirt.

Shirley concentrated on her plants and pretended to hear what this blowhard had to say to her.

"Go ahead," Shirley said plainly, regretting she permitted him to speak.

"Sorry to intrude like this," LaForge replied sheepishly. "I- I've tried to call you, but you don't answer your phone."

No response came from Shirley, only the noise of her digging with her decent-sized hand trowel.

"Anyway, I wanted to talk with you about your property taxes. I was in the neighborhood, and I thought I would stop by and —"

Shirley rose from her kneeling position and moved away from her plants. She removed her flowery-designed cloth apron and jersey gardening gloves and laid them next to the flower bed.

"Well, I am off to take my morning walk," stated Shirley.

"Do you mind if I join you?"

Shirley looked incredulously at the well-dressed LaForge.

"You want to walk with me? In that?" Shirley said, pointing at LaForge's state of dress.

"Oh yes, I have time before I have to get to work, and besides, I could use the exercise."

She looked at him for a moment. *This should be interesting*, she thought and shrugged her shoulders.

"Well, come on then," Shirley replied, murmuring.

Shirley and LaForge set off along a path away from the house and the main dirt road.

"It seems like you have been in arrears on this property for some time now."

"Oh?"

"Why, yes. We would keep sending you letters regarding this issue, but that doesn't seem very effective," LaForge said with a forced smile.

Shirley didn't respond to LaForge, nor did she even want to deal with this annoying man. She regretted allowing him to disrupt her usually tranquil walk.

"Well, I also wanted to bring a personal touch. We're such a small town, and I've never seen you around. I wanted to meet you face to face."

"Well, now you've seen me," Shirley replied, clearly annoyed.

"Mrs. Chapman? May I call you Mrs. Chapman?"

"If you like."

"I don't know if you know the gravity of not paying your property taxes," said LaForge gravely.

"I've lived in this house for over fifty years. I own this house. Haven't I paid enough property tax?" Shirley said, her voice laced with contempt.

"Well, no. You see, it doesn't matter how long you've

lived here."

"No?"

"No. You see, we need property tax for our roads, our schools, you know, things like that."

"I don't use the roads very much, and I'm too old to go to school."

"I wish there was a way we could work this out. What about your spouse?"

"My husband was sent to heaven some time ago."

"I see. You don't have any family that could help?"

"They live far away from me and don't need to be bothered with this."

"That's a shame. I wouldn't want you to lose your beautiful house."

The grandmother looked at LaForge and the path ahead — nothing but grass and soil and a few small saplings.

"You might want to walk on this side. The ground is pretty soft over there," Shirley gently coaxed.

LaForge moved to where she indicated, but the ground gave way underneath him as he did. His feet sank into the soil.

"Mrs. Chapman. Mrs. Chapman!" LaForge cried.

LaForge tried to get his feet out of the soft ground, but sank even further as he struggled.

"Mrs. Chapman. I'm sinking. I- I can't get out. You need to help me," LaForge said, whining.

The grandmother stared at him with a steely gaze, daring not to lift a finger to help this insufferable man.

"You can't do this. HELP!" LaForge screamed.

LaForge struggled but couldn't escape this thick, black

mud pit now sunk to his thighs. He reached for a small branch on a sapling with two hands and tugged on it to get himself out. Shirley removed a pair of pruning shears from her pocket, leaned across, and cut the small branch, leaving LaForge holding a severed, useless tree branch. He dropped it and stared wide-eyed at Shirley as the mud was caking up upon his thighs.

"Don't do this. Don't let me die like this. We can work something out. Please..." begged LaForge.

Shirley did nothing and appeared extremely annoyed that LaForge took so long for the mud to envelop his body. Something caught LaForge's attention, and he looked ahead in awe and fright.

"Oh my God!" he said.

A creature stood nearby and looked at Shirley and LaForge, who struggled desperately with fresh intent in the soft soil, with it now reaching his waist.

"What is that?" LaForge cried.

The creature lowered himself into the soft ground and disappeared below it. LaForge's panic kicked into overdrive as he scrambled to desperately but uselessly free himself from the darkened mud. Suddenly, tentacles emerged from the black around him and grabbed his waist and arms. The tentacles encircled him. Two clawed hands rose from the soil and raked and tore at LaForge's torso and head. LaForge screamed in pain and terror as the tentacles and hands pulled him further and further down into the blackened mire. The softened sludge filled LaForge's mouth and muffled his screams before his head was pulled down below the surface of the soil. The mud smoothed itself, returned to its normal state, and then silence. A smile of satisfaction crossed Shirley's face as she resumed her walk amongst the estate grounds.

SEVEN

"They have been wonderful companions, but things have changed," Shirley stated as she ended her story, and time shifted back to the present.

"Changed?" Alexis said.

"Oh, how I've missed you, and the Mal un Marais have missed you, too. But now, they're not sad… no… they're angry. They want to keep you here… for good," Shirley replied.

"Because I left?" said Alexis, trying to get her head around her grandmother's story about these strange creatures and the relationship she allegedly had with them.

"Of course. They are a part of you. They… they saved you," Shirley stated.

"Saved me?" Alexis replied, wondering if this figment of her grandmother was in her right mind or if she was all dreaming this somehow.

"Yes. They saved you. I saved you," Shirley said plainly, without a hint of boasting. "You may not remember, but they saved me and you."

"Why me?" asked Alexis.

"Because I was desperate. Because you were my favorite. Because you had the sight. Like me."

Puzzled and nervous, Alexis rose from the floor and backed away from her grandmother, not believing anything in the specter before her. *This isn't real. I know it can't be.*

"Alexis, where are you going?" cried Shirley.

"I- I don't know what you're talking about. I- I wasn't saved by anyone or anything," Alexis said, her voice trembling.

"Yes, you were. I know it was a traumatic event, but you must have come to terms with it by now," assured Shirley.

"I- I haven't."

"It must be them. Be careful of them. They can deceive you. They always have and always will. They've done it to me."

"I- I don't believe any of this. I wasn't saved. I don't have what you say I have. I don't have this sight! I'm nothing special!" said Alexis, her voice rising in panic and fear.

Alexis ran away from her grandmother, opened the door, and entered the hallway, leaving the spirit behind.

"You are!" Shirley called out. "You are special! Never deny what you are!"

Alexis saw Kim in the hallway, went to her, and embraced her tightly.

"Where have you been?" Kim cried, breaking away from her sister's hug.

"I just talked with grandma," Alexis said with a shudder.

A creature oozed out of the hallway wall and emerged

into the hallway; its sights set upon the two sisters. The beast slowly began their advance.

"Grandma?" Kim replied with skepticism.

"Listen, we don't have much time. We have to get out of here. Out of this house," Alexis said in a tone of panic as she looked at the creature in the hallway.

The creature stopped its advance, raised its foot, and slammed it onto the floor—an enormous crack formed in the floorboards that traveled underneath Alexis and Kim, who felt the force and the unstable foundation underneath them.

"C'mon Kim! We have to go! We have to go now!" Alexis said in a panic.

Alexis tried to pull Kim away from the danger they faced in the hallway, but Kim remained rooted in her space. Alexis' powerful force was no match for Kim's immovable object. Puzzled, she looked into Kim's eyes and saw tears streaming down her face as she began to weep.

"I- I can't," Kim said in a near whisper. "You've always tried to protect me, and I'll always love you for that. It- It's too —"

The creature raised its foot and slammed it into the floor yet again. The floorboards beneath them gave way, and Alexis and Kim fell through the floorboards and into a water-filled cellar. After what seemed to be ages, Alexis surfaced and frantically looked for Kim.

"Kim? Kim!" said Alexis, her voice echoing off the walls.

Alexis trod water, turned, and dunked her head underwater in every direction. After many attempts of dunking and resurfacing, she was unsuccessful in her attempts to find Kim, yelling her sister's name every time she was able to get oxygen into her lungs.

Suddenly, a bloated, decomposed body bobbed up in front of Alexis, and she screamed in terror at the unexpected sight of it. Then another waterlogged corpse popped up out of the water, followed by another, totaling three swollen, rotted bodies surrounding her. She screamed and did her damnedest in the deep water to push them away, but they kept coming back to her as if they were iron bars and Alexis was the magnet. One body rolled over to her left, and Kim's decayed face confronted her. Alexis turned her head to the right, away from Kim's corpse, only to see Dante's bloated face on one of the other corpses. When Alexis moved her eyes to the front, she saw Jan's putrefied face. The three bodies bobbed and converged on Alexis, who tried to fight and push them away, but their attraction to her was far too strong for Alexis to make a space for herself. During this battle, Alexis struggled to keep her head above the water's surface as she continued her attempts to push the bodies away. Alexis began to tire and weaken with each push and ounce of energy. The bodies that were surrounding her began to pile themselves upon the top of Alexis' head, forcing her under the dark water.

Alexis continued her struggle to escape from the bodies, but they remained with her and forced her deeper and deeper down into the numbing, cold water. Alexis stopped struggling with her arms going limp, a signal of surrender as her mouth opened and expelled the final amount of oxygen contained in her lungs—her last bubbles of life. She looked up one final time and, beyond the bodies, saw a hand thrust down into the water. Alexis turned her surrender into determination, pushed up through the bodies, and swam toward the hand. Through the water, she saw a distorted view of her grandmother leaning over the side of a boat with two other figures. She reached out and touched the hand. The hand wrapped around hers pulled her speedily out of the water through the cellar's ceiling and dumped her body onto the upper-level bathroom floor.

Alexis, on her hands and knees, spewed and coughed water from her lungs and onto the floor as she tried to recover from her crazed nightmare, along with the failed attempt at drowning. She caught her breath and looked around, realizing she was alone. No voices, no footsteps — nothing at all. The echoing of a dripping tap was the only sound Alexis could hear as she shivered with cold and fear. Picking up the rhythm of the dripping sound, Alexis slowly turned her head towards the bathtub. Suddenly, tentacles appeared over the bathtub's edge, and a clawed hand rose from the clawfoot tub, its fingers curled around the edge. As the clawed hand pulled itself out of the tub, the head of the creature appeared. Its wide black eyes and moss-filled face decorated its oversized cranium with its fangs jutting out of its large black slit of a mouth. The Creature rose to its full height and stepped out of the bathtub. It towered over Alexis, who screamed and scrambled to her feet as she stumbled out of the bathroom, the creature giving chase.

Alexis ran down the long hallway with the creature in quick pursuit. Its heavy footfalls shook the floorboards, threatening Alexis's balance as she ran. Alexis got to the door, opened it, and ran outside. She ran across the front yard straight into the arms of the local sheriff. He was a pasty, heavy-set bull of a man in his mid-forties, and his deputy, who displayed the same pasty texture but fewer years and pounds than his boss, stood a few paces behind.

"Whoa! Whoa! What's going on here?" the sheriff said.

"Some- something is chasing me!" said Alexis in exhaustion and near collapse.

"What? What's chasing you?" the sheriff said, his speech quickening.

"A Mal in- a Mal un Marais!" Alexis replied, trying to tear herself away from the officer.

"A Mal un Marais?" the deputy said.

"It's right behind me and —"

Alexis struggled to turn back and pointed weakly at the house, but saw only an empty doorway. She took several steps from the officers, turned her head around nervously, and viewed the area where their cars were parked, but Alexis only saw her rental car. It was as if her sibling's vehicles never existed here.

"But- but there was…Where are the…"

"What's a Mal un Marais?" the deputy asked the sheriff.

"I've heard of it. Some silly lore. An old wives' tale."

"No. It's not. I swear," said Alexis as she turned to confront the officers.

"Girl, you are soaking wet," stated the sheriff, inspecting Alexis' disheveled form.

"I know. I- I was in a cellar filled with water."

"A cellar?" the sheriff said, his face creased in skepticism.

"Yes sir, a cellar. It's right below the main floor of the house, and there was —"

"That's impossible," the sheriff stated.

"No, I'm serious there is —"

"Ma'am. There can't be a cellar," the deputy said, cutting her off. "We're below sea level."

"Wait... what?"

"We're below sea level," the sheriff replied, repeating the reality. "If anyone even started to dig down into this ground, all they would get would be a hole filled with water."

"See the cemetery over there?" said the deputy, pointing to the skyline and to the right, which revealed, in the distance, a small cemetery can be seen.

"All the graves in that cemetery are above ground for the reason we gave you," the sheriff replied deadpan.

"What- what are you doing here?" Alexis asked, not believing what she was hearing.

"We were doing our community patrol and saw your car. It didn't look familiar to us."

"Wait... you're Shirley Chapman's granddaughter, aren't you?" asked the sheriff, looking at her closely and examining Alexis up and down.

"Yes."

As the sheriff and the deputy continued to examine her more intensely, Alexis felt something creep down the base of her skull and slither slowly down each vertebra of her back. These law enforcement agents seemed to objectify her, but she felt something different... even sinister.

"Oh my God. You're Alexis," the deputy stated.

"Yes," Alexis replied nervously.

"Wow. It's been a long time. You've grown," the sheriff said.

Alexis stared at them with a puzzled and frightened look.

"Where is your grandmother?" the deputy asked.

"She… she's…" Alexis stuttered, unable to frame the correct words for the madness she experienced.

The sheriff and the deputy looked at each other. Their suspicion grew as their eyes examined the grounds and the enormous residence.

"We better have a look."

The sheriff and the deputy moved toward the front door. Alexis stood there, frozen, knowing what she should do — flee.

"Miss… Alexis? Please come with us and check out the house."

§

The sheriff and the deputy entered and scanned the entry hall with Alexis trailing behind. Trash bags and cleaning supplies were strewn about the hallway.

"This… something is wrong," Alexis said.

"Mrs. Chapman!" the deputy called out.

"Shirley?" the sheriff said in a loud voice.

The three of them went down the hallway. A gigantic drop of water fell and landed on the back of the sheriff's broad shoulders. He looked up and saw an enormous dark water stain on the ceiling.

"Is there a bathroom upstairs?" the sheriff asked Alexis.

"No," Alexis replied in a low voice.

"Looks like you've got a leak," the deputy stated.

The sheriff and the deputy continued down the hallway. Alexis looked back up at the ceiling where the water stain had disappeared.

"Sheriff, take a look at this," the deputy said, his tone grave.

The deputy pointed to the floor down the hallway. A

small stream of water rippled and moved across it like a reptilian sidewinder. The sheriff and the deputy moved closer as the water seeped beneath a door.

"What room is this?" said the deputy to Alexis.

"The bathroom," Alexis replied.

"Did you leave something on?" asked the sheriff.

Alexis shook her head in the negative. The ssheriff and the deputy opened the bathroom door and found the floor utterly wet with water. They entered the bathroom and heard the faucet rushing water into the bathtub. The sheriff and the deputy moved closer and peered into the tub to find Shirley Chapman's dead, bloated body that had been submerged in the water for what seemed to be an eternity. The deputy stepped forward and turned off the faucet. Alexis approached and saw her grandmother's frail, decayed body and cried out in shock. She felt the glare of the sheriff and the deputy boring into her back.

"No... This didn't happen," Alexis said. "I didn't do this! My grandmother is already dead!"

"What do you mean she's already dead?" the sheriff replied, his tone firm.

"I- I came to this house after her funeral," Alexis said in a trembling tone.

"Her funeral? When was that?" the sheriff asked.

"Well, it was... it was...a couple of months ago. It was sudden. My siblings were there. My brother Dante, his wife Jan, and my sister Kim," Alexis said, shuddering at her confession.

The sheriff and the deputy looked at each other, their faces a mixture of skepticism and bewilderment. Alexis thought about what she just said. *These officers think I'm crazy! The truth is the goddamn truth!*

"Ma'am, I think you need to come outside with us," said the deputy in a grave tone.

The sheriff and the deputy grabbed Alexis by the arms and walked her toward the bathroom door.

"No, I'm telling you, she's already dead. I came to this house with my brother, sister, and sister-in-law," Alexis cried, desperately trying to convince the lawmen.

Her pleas were for naught as the sheriff and the deputy continued to escort Alexis down the long, shadowy hallway with Alexis struggling and kicking in a desperate effort to break the grip of the men.

"No, really," Alexis said in desperation.

"It can't be," the sheriff replied, his voice hard as stone.

"No, I'm telling you it's true and —"

"Your family died in this house roughly nine years ago," the deputy stated.

"They drowned," the sheriff said. "All of them."

"Wait, what?"

"A hurricane about nine years ago," said the sheriff. "They were all swept away…… wiped out. Your father, mother, sister, brother, sister-in-law… everybody."

"No… they —"

"You and your grandmother were the only survivors," the deputy said, adding more information. "We rescued you in a boat."

Alexis tried to open her mouth, but nothing came out, only tears and cries of anguish.

"We were in the boat with you," said the sheriff.

The sheriff and deputy continued to pull Alexis down the hallway, through the door, and out into the front of the house. Alexis finally broke free from their grasp as they crossed the front yard and turned to confront them. She opened her mouth to speak, but as she did so, the beings of the sheriff and the deputy, like a TV channel with bad reception, flickered between human and creature form. Alexis blinked in disbelief.

"All the houses were destroyed in this area except for this one," the sheriff said formally, his form continually shifting.

Alexis shook her head to clear these visions, but the human/creature form of the sheriff and the deputy's shapes continued to flicker, shuttling from human to inhuman. The sheriff and the deputy sensed this from Alexis.

"We punish, too," said the Deputy Creature.

"Wha- what?" Alexis said, her voice stammering.

"In the book that your grandmother made you read to her, it never stated that our jobs in Hell are demons who punish people's souls?" the Sheriff Creature asked.

"That's why your sight has gotten a glimpse of our work," the Deputy Creature said.

"Just a glimpse, mind you, just a glimpse, as the punishment is repeated over and over and over again," the Sheriff Creature stated, his lips curled in a grin.

"Some people's sight is so strong it can make other people view these punishments," said the Deputy Creature.

"We save the good ones for them," stated the Sheriff Creature.

The Sheriff Creature and the Deputy Creature laughed sadistically in a low, warbled tone, enjoying the rewards of their work.

"No…" Alexis said, her voice a tone of pleading.

"But we couldn't punish your sister's soul like we wanted to," Sheriff Creature said with a snide.

"Thanks to you," stated the Deputy Creature.

"But it was all taken care of," the Sheriff Creature replied.

Alexis' head jerked up, and an image flashed into her mind, adding to this nightmare…

§

Kim was on her knees at the cellar door, shaking. Her face was streaming wet with tears. She heard the pounding from the cellar door. Tears ran non-stop down her cheeks. She gripped the broken key in her shaking hand and stared at the destroyed object with her blurred vision. Her head moved back and forth from the key to the door like some broken stringed marionette.

§

"We didn't have to do a thing," the Sheriff Creature said in a flattened tone.

"Yeah, easy work. She's crippled. Drowning in her guilt," the Deputy Creature replied with a giggle.

"We just kick back, relax, and watch them punish themselves again and again. Over and over. It's got to be the worst punishment I've ever seen," the Sheriff Creature stated.

"Looks like you failed her, too. Just like Krystal," the Deputy Creature replied with a slight chortle.

The Sheriff and Deputy Creatures laughed in unison, enjoying their torments.

"Your grandmother could have evacuated like everyone else in this area when the hurricane came," said the Sheriff Creature.

"But she decided to wait it out," the Deputy Creature stated. "Your parents were so concerned for your grandmother's safety that they stayed with her."

"They also brought you, your brother, and your sister along," said the Sheriff Creature.

"That's when she prayed for the house and for you to be saved," replied the Deputy Creature.

"Since she loved this house so much, we decided that her soul should never leave it," the Sheriff Creature said with a brag.

"No... no!" Alexis cried.

The Creatures stabilized back into the form of the sheriff and the deputy.

"Ma'am, we need to take you down to the station for questioning," the sheriff said.

The sheriff and the deputy grabbed Alexis. They shoved the struggling Alexis against the patrol car and attempted to handcuff her. As Alexis struggled with the two burly officers, she looked at one of the bedroom windows. She saw the apparition of her grandmother. Her grandmother violently shook her head 'no' at Alexis from the bedroom window. Alexis' eyes shot open and flashed, and she saw what had happened to her grandmother...

§

With her back against the door and her face bloodied, Shirley slumped to the floor. She drew her breath quickly, as though in pain, and lifted her hand, which was swelling and becoming bloated in front of her eyes.

"No... NO!"

She felt her face with her oversized hand, and she also

found it swollen. Shirley's face contorted in panic as large shadows cast over her. She looked up. A green substance dripped onto her face from the shadows. Her eyes grew wide, and she screamed in terror as two clawed hands lifted Shirley by her arms and dragged her down the hallway. Shirley turned to view the two Mal un Marais and into their black-eyed, bog-mossed countenances. Shirley struggled to escape their grip, but her efforts were futile. The creatures dragged her into the bathroom, one of them taking its gigantic, clawed hand that turned the cross-handled fixtures on the front of the bathtub. The faucet quickly filled the sizeable, aged porcelain vessel as Shirley struggled with the other shaggy, lichened beast, desperate to break its grip.

"Please! Let me go!" Shirley begged.

The creatures lifted her and dropped her into the bathtub. Shirley struggled to escape the tub, but the creatures held her down. As the tub continued to fill up with the water, beginning to level up to the tub's edge, the creatures pushed her shoulders down, forcing her head under the water. Shirley clawed at their arms and pushed her head above the water to gulp in the air at the surface. Suddenly, Shirley released her grip on them and clutched at her chest. The creatures released their grip on her and watched the panicked look on her face as she slid under the water, her eyes begging for help, but the creatures provided none, ignoring her pleas. Shirley's mouth spasmed as she tried in vain to suck in oxygen, but her lungs were replaced with water from the tub. The last air left in her body bubbled out as her heart gave out. Shirley's white-knuckled hands released their grip on her chest and floated above her, lifeless. The creatures watched momentarily, then shapeshifted into the sheriff and the deputy. The sheriff took a two-way radio from his belt, held it up, and pushed the transmit button on the radio.

§

Alexis snapped back to the present, still struggling with the sheriff and the deputy as they tried to get the handcuffs on her.

"We called it in. We knew that you would come," the sheriff stated in his creature voice.

"She was old. We wanted someone new. Someone young. And you are so young and pretty. She promised us that if we saved the house and you when the hurricane swept everything away, you would be given to us," replied the Deputy in his creature voice.

"Our prize. We have missed you so much," the sheriff said, tears welling in his eyes.

Alexis found strength in her and broke free from their clutches. She spun to the side, quickly snatched the gun from the sheriff's holster, and stepped back to confront them. The deputy reached for his gun, but Alexis swung the barrel to his head. The deputy stopped, backed away, and raised his hands in the air away from his gun. The creatures transformed into their human voices.

"Ma'am… put the gun down," the sheriff said calmly.

"No!" Alexis exclaimed as she swung the gun at the sheriff and then back to the deputy.

"Ma'am, you heard the sheriff. Put the gun down. You're already in enough —"

BANG!

The deputy grabbed his chest as the bullet from the gun

slammed into his torso. He staggered and fell to the ground.

BANG!

The bullet blasted through the sheriff's collarbone, shattering it. He howled in pain and fell flat on his back. Alexis looked in stunned silence at what she had just done. She threw the gun to the ground and ran off toward the rented SUV. The sheriff and the deputy lay there, with the gun inert between them, as the sound of Alexis' car engine revved to life, followed by the sound of wheels spinning on the dirt as a car accelerated away and into the distance before the sound slowly faded. The sheriff and the deputy rolled and squirmed in the soft soil, followed by moans of pain emanating out of their mouths. Suddenly, the moist ground vibrated, and the sheriff and the deputy began to sink into the darkened earth. They screamed and shrieked in their mixture of human and creature voices as the ground swallowed them up along with their patrol car. The sheriff and deputy's shrieks become muffled and then silenced as the ground closed above them, never to resurface again.

EIGHT

A TENTACLE WRAPPED AROUND THE JAR OF KEYS ABANDONED in the bedroom. The tentacle lifted the jar of keys to an enormously clawed hand. Heavy footsteps bounced in a rhythm as the Mal un Marais descended the stairs. Its clawed hand and mossy arm cradled the jar of keys. As the creature made its destination to the ground floor, its clawed hand put the jar of keys on one of the shelves in the kitchen. A diffused, distorted reflection of the creature courtesy of the dusty, elongated, massive mason jar—the holder of the keys. The creature walked out of the kitchen. He and his brethren then went to ground — hoping, praying that someone would inhabit this now lonely house.

§

Alexis bounced around the interior cabin of her rental SUV as her foot was heavy on the accelerator. *Fuck the seatbelt! I have to get the hell out of there!* As the SUV's suspension was getting a workout over the uneven dirt road, Alexis's head slammed into the roof of the car, dazing her slightly, but she kept driving. As she came to the end of the dirt road and onto a paved one, her foot on the pedal never lightened as the SUV climbed up the small hill and onto the asphalt. She continued to floor it until she reached her destination—the hotel that was away from that damned house! With her luck, a real officer would pull her over for speeding, not wearing a seatbelt, reckless driving, blah, blah. She continued to drive, and luck was on her side. As her travel went uninterrupted, she quickly pulled into a parking space, pushed the automatic shifter to park, and turned off the ignition. She placed her forehead on the steering wheel and took deep breaths in an attempt to abate her anxiety. *You're okay. You survived*, Alexis would repeat in her head. She touched herself to check if she was still here and not some shade from the estate. *You're still here. You're good.* When Alexis finally convinced herself that she was present and her anxiety lessened to a point where she could function somewhat normally, she pushed the car door open and made her exit.

§

The hotel room door opened, and Alexis entered. She pushed the hotel door shut with her back and took a deep breath to calm herself. A loud buzzing vibrated from her front pants pocket as she blew her breath out. She fished out her phone and looked at the number. Her brow furrowed in confusion. It wasn't a number she knew, but it looked familiar. She punched the answer number with her index finger and the speaker icon.

"H-hello."

"Hi, is this Alexis? Alexis DeLong?"

"Yes."

"This is Wynn Stonecipher. I'm the lawyer who handled your grandmother's will. I've been trying to get ahold of you all day."

"Yeah, well, I've been over at her house cleaning and—"

"Well, that's what I wanted to discuss with you. Some urgent issues have come up, and I need to speak with you about them. Are you free this afternoon?"

"I don't know, I—"

"Perfect. How does around 4:00 sound?"

§

Alexis sat on a mahogany chair made for function rather than comfort. Across the gigantic desk of the same material sat Stonecipher, a tall, thin man with a thick but graying head of hair, which was terrific for a man in his mid-fifties. His large palms with long fingers made each of his hands look like spiders. His face was handsome, with his blue-gray eyes and pronounced aquiline nose providing some pleasant features, a stark change to the horrid monstrosities she encountered at the house.

"Glad you could come in and see me," Wynn said with a smile, speaking quickly with a slight. "You said you visited the house, and you were cleaning it, correct?"

"Yes."

"Well, I wouldn't bother anymore. I have some new information."

"Oh?"

"Did you see any papers or letters in the house when you were there?"

"I saw some mail and letters around the house, but I

didn't open them or—"

"Those letters were bills for property taxes that have been in arrears for some time."

"Oh," said Alexis in a quiet tone. She knew this, but how would she tell Wynn? That her ghost told her the bills weren't paid? Wynn would draw up commitment papers for her to sign, which she would have considered.

"Due to the unpaid taxes, the house is now underwater."

When Wynn said his last word, which became distorted in Alexis' mind, her brain went back to the basement where she nearly drowned with the corpses of her family dragging her down and, when she looked up to see her grandmother's warped hand at the surface, up from her almost watery grave.

"Miss DeLong? Anna?"

Hearing Wynn's quick but pleasant voice snapped her out of her daymare, feeling a tear stream down her cheek.

"Are you okay?" Wynn asked as concern crept upon his face.

"I'm fine, I'm fine," Alexis replied, brushing away the tear. "You said my grandmother's house is—"

"Underwater. It means that you owe more than the estate is worth. So cleaning it up would be pointless as you wouldn't be able to sell it unless you can come up with the money to satisfy the debt."

"How much is the debt?" Alexis asked.

"About four to five million dollars since the property taxes haven't been paid in ages. Someone fell asleep at the wheel at city hall."

"Yeah, I can't afford that," said Alexis.

"I would let it fall into foreclosure. That way, the bank

can take over the property, fix it up, and sell it to recover their losses." Wynn stated as he shuffled through the papers on his desk, found what he needed, and placed the paper in front of Alexis. "I just need you to sign a foreclosure agreement to let the bank take your grandmother's estate over."

Alexis looked at the paper, which seemed straightforward, at least what she could decipher. She could never translate legalese and knew none of her friends could. She took the pen and started to write her signature.

"Too bad that the house isn't haunted," Wynn said in an attempt at a joke. "The property value would go way up."

Alexis forced a weak smile as she finished her signature. She would never return to the house and hoped that the jar that started this madness was thrown away in the nearest landfill, never to be discovered again.

§

The jar of keys remained on the shelf as time passed. It was in continual movement as the days rolled past. A beam of daylight swept rapidly across the shelf. A little more dust was on the jar as each day passed around the surrounding shelf. Nighttime. Daytime. After some time had passed, warped reflections of many construction workers and tradespeople came into view of the jar carrying tools and lumber. The noise of work surrounded the house. The whine of a power saw. The thud of a hammer. As the workers restored the neglected house daily, more and more keys appeared in the jar, like someone storing their loose change. A beam of daylight swept along the shelf but stopped on the jar, its contents filled to the brim, recording each day of vacancy.

The jar and the surrounding shelf were spotless, with

cleaners picking up and polishing every inch of square footage, including the old antique jar. Suddenly, the sound of an essential turning in the lock on the front door opened it. Footsteps approached, and clear, concise reflections of a slim, attractive Caucasian woman in her early thirties entered the foyer. Behind her, a young couple, a handsome man and a beautiful woman, appeared in the jar, the personification of the perfect couple, both in their mid-twenties. The realtor stopped and looked down the long hallway adjacent to the kitchen while the couple looked around the place while remaining in the foyer—a plasticine smile molded upon her face.

"You're going to love this place."

THE END

ACKNOWLEDGMENTS

I want to thank the following people who helped me through this haunted house-creature feature mashup—A. A. Medina, who did a phenomenal job on this novella's cover art and formatting. Candace Nola, Mort Stone, and 360 Editing (a division of Uncomfortably Dark Horror) for their expert editing, for which I am forever thankful, and, as always, my "wife" Lisa Branum, whose encouragement has made me forge ahead despite the odds. I appreciate all of you!

ABOUT THE AUTHOR

Paul Grammatico resides in the San Francisco Bay Area. *Keys of Demented Memories* is his third book and fourth published story. Paul is an avid fan of cult movies and books of various genres. He is working on a short story collection, a western, and a sports/horror novel.

When he isn't reading, writing, or being a hockey maven, he watches serial TV shows with his significant other, Lisa, and their four cats.

Paul can be found on the following platforms:

Twitter (X): @paul_grammatico

Instagram: @paulgrammatico

Facebook: https://www.facebook.com/paulgramm66

BOOKS BY THE AUTHOR

Starvation Lake

Five hunters head up to Northern Michigan in the dead of winter during deer hunting season in a desolate place called Starvation Lake. When a horrifying accident occurs, leaving an elderly woman fatally wounded with no help in sight and then covering up their crime in the deep snow. In its aftermath, the hunters face numerous perils in the surrounding pristine woods, which begin to turn on them. As the hunters' lives are in jeopardy, they realize that the dead woman's words are not a plea but a curse.

Now on Amazon!

Insects of the Damned

Many strange things happen in a small town, but for local law enforcement and an eccentric scientist, this was more than they bargained for in their town of Mintonka, Minnesota. An insect invasion in a small farming town cuts a swath of gruesome terror. A group of locals join forces to locate the cause of how these insects are alive, how their carnivorous tendencies came about, and what can be done to destroy them.

Now on Amazon!

Lies with Monsters

A tabloid journalist meets a shadowy figure in a back alley in Los Angeles. The figure tells her tale of being a porn actor turned streetwalker turned starlet. The journalist and the figure have parallels in their lives with the rise and fall of their careers, but the endgame between them results in a bizarre and bloodstained climax of chaos and revenge.

Now on Godless.com!